TURN LEFT I THINK.

A Farming Life.
Brown Owl.
Cold Water Swimming.
Señorita.
Academic Success At Last.
Fun On The Water.
Red Rover.
Bombed Out London.
The Big Freeze.
First Love.
I'm Cornish Now.
Runaways.
Working.
Life In A Bubble.
On The Road.
A Life At Sea.
Not Henley-on-Thames.
A Blonde Ukrainian Man.
Another Beautiful Cities, Gone Now.
Egyptian border.
No Remorse.
Escape.
Coup d'etat, Not Ice Cream.
Turned on.
Going Home.
West End Club.
The Forbidden City.
A School Girl.
City Of Bridges.

Money Change/Life Change.
Donkey Business.
A Night At The Opera.
A Strange Happening in Omonia Square.
Goodbye Friends.
Breaking-up is Hard To Do.
Polska Piękność.
Marry Me.
The Bus.
Exhausted.
Flying Tesserae.
Sheepskins From Istanbul.
Shirts from Marrakesh.
Reading Rock Festival.
Ireland, Safe From The Atom Bomb
Life on the Thames.
Poland.
Doctor Ali's Afghan Sheepskin Coats.
A Home At Last.
The Family Dog Shop.
Unrecognised Genius.
The Road to Goulimine.
Reverse Property Development.
A Diplomatic Incident.
A Strange Incident In Gretna Green.
A Study On Where Time Goes.

A Farming Life.

I hear nothing and I see nothing but I feel. I feel a sense of warmth and perhaps pain, a sucking sensation. I am aware of a fight, a struggle. A fight for breath and a fight for life. But I am not alone. I am doing this with someone, someone who cares, someone who knows what they are doing and someone who will fight for my survival. I fill my lungs with fresh oxygen and I cry out, as loud as I can. The pain subsides and is replaced with an overwhelming hunger. I search for sustenance in desperation, I find it and I suck. I have been born. I was born suffering from hyperthymesia but I will soon be able to overcome it with a good diet and plenty of exercise.

One Friday evening, just before my bedtime, my Dad informed me that we would be going to the countryside tomorrow and staying on a farm for a few days. I wasn't sure what the countryside was but I knew what a farm was. I had seen pictures of cows, pigs and chickens so I was pretty genned up on the subject. Having a good analytical mind I figured out that farms, rather than being located among lots of houses, streets and lorries, were probably in the countryside, so it sounded like a good place to go.

We arrived at uncle Emlyn's farm around lunch time on Saturday. The first thing I noticed was the wonderful smell. I was told it was poo, but I knew that it didn't smell anything like poo. I was glad it was lunch time, because I had only had a rusk since breakfast and I was starving. It was a huge house with a large kitchen and a stove, with lunch, I hope mine, bubbling on the top. After lunch I was taken upstairs, past the grandfather clock on the landing, to a room the size of our house. This was to be my bedroom so I settled down for a well earned afternoon nap.

After my nap I started to explore the farm yard. There were chickens running around, goats in a pen and a nice lady, with the rather strange name of Milkmaid, doing something to the underside of a huge cow and a galvanised bucket. As I walked past she poured me a cup of milk so I wondered if that had anything to do with her name. Later I was introduced to a baby goat called Scapegoat, another strange name, but I was in a foreign country called Welsh, so strange words were to be expected. I was asked to feed Scapegoat with a bottle which I was happy to do and quite experienced in handling a bottle, although I hadn't used one for some months now. For the rest of our stay Scapegoat followed me everywhere, including all over the house, although he was not allowed to go up to my bedroom.

During my first night I was woken in the middle of the night, around seven, by this monster bellowing and bashing against the wall so hard I could feel the walls vibrating. I was so terrified it took me a further fifteen minutes to get back to sleep. In the morning I talked about my fear of this monster, and Uncle Emlyn said "Come with me Paul, it's time for you to meet Tank the bull." Tank was corralled in a small area in a corner just outside of my bedroom, and he really was a monster. Apparently he gave no milk, so I was never sure why they kept him.

The following night I was woken again, which was odd because I was told it was peaceful in the countryside. This time it was voices and lights and my Mum came to my bedroom and said I could get dressed and come outside and watch. There were lots of people outside in the dark, some holding torches. Uncle Emlyn and my Dad were heaving on a rope tied to something, I have no idea what, sticking out the bottom of a cow. After much bellowing, heaving and grunting a slimy body flopped on the grass. Within minutes it had transformed into a calf and was standing up, being licked by its Mum. I said "I know how you feel." to the calf and went to bed for another twelve hours sleep.

The following morning I was working in the hay barn with my brother and Scapegoat. Uncle Emlyn had given us the job of building a castle in the haystack. As if we didn't have enough work on, he further tasked us with looking after seven young border collie puppies. We got on well with our work until lunchtime when I was horrified to realise we had misplaced one of the puppies. I was so afraid I would not be given any more serious work in the future. Fortunately a full scale search party involving the whole family soon found the missing puppy.

At the end of the week I was informed tomorrow would be going-home time. What! I was mortified. I thought this was a permanent move and that I would be living and working on the farm forever. "Who will take care of Scapegoat?" I demanded. I was told Milkmaid would look after him very well. I was still not happy with this proposal to go home, and used all the powers of persuasion at my disposal to alter this ridiculous decision. Even the deployment of logic failed to change Mum's mind, possibly because I was not yet four. In a final last ditch attempt I threw myself in the mud and thrashed around wildly but still no change of plan. What is wrong with these people?

Brown Owl.

School was strange for me. Not particularly happy, yet not unhappy. My primary school, St. Michael's Preparatory School, was a private school in Woking, run by two octogenarians in a wonderful Victorian mansion. Mrs. Roberts would run the school, and Mr. Roberts would run the kitchen. Meals would always comprise roast meat, with ample helpings of fat and gristle, potato and cabbage, followed by a small jam tart. Of course we had the statutory two milk breaks throughout the day, at which we would receive the standard government issue (GI) of a glass bottle containing a third of a pint of full-fat milk. According to a government investigation, drinking milk would help children perform better at school. I tried it, but it didn't work.

The education was carried out by a male and a female teacher. Mr Johnson was tough. He was not long back from a stint with the *Forgotten Army* in Burma. Under Lieutenant General Slim of the Fourteenth Army, he was involved in the successful defeat of the Japanese Army at the *Battle of Admin Box*. This was a vital base for the resupply by aircraft of cut off units. He talked about his wartime experiences often. During physical education periods we would be marched around the grounds waiting for him to shout "melt". At this command we were expected to fall into ditches, hedgerow or puddles in order to avoid the marauding Japanese troops, of which there were few in Woking.

One lunch time, I decided it would be fun, and I would gain kudos if I were to bend the lead pipe from the hand-washing basin so it flooded the courtyard. Sixty odd pupils washing their hands before lunch, which was obligatory, did the trick. The whole school had to go to the assembly hall, which was in fact the old parquet floored billiard hall, to be given the chance to do the honourable thing and own up. There followed ten minutes of looking around as if trying to blame someone else for a fart. Clearly I was not honourable.

When this failed to reveal the culprit, he announced "Tenko". Tenko was a Japanese word, used in the prisoner of war camps, and loosely translates as roll-call. So we were all moved to the courtyard and told to stand there, in the sun, until the delinquent, me, came forward. He marched up and down getting more and more agitated as I became more determined not to give in. Eventually he gave up, he had to, and I had won.

Outside of school, I would play in the street, like everyone else. Trying to climb up the stink pole, which was a kind of rite of passage that I never managed to achieve. In and out of other people's houses and lives. Older brothers were going off to do their National Service, practising in their skiffle groups, buying their first motorbike or air pistol. Jim's older brother, with his first air pistol, jokingly pointed it at my face, saying it wasn't loaded and pulled the trigger. It was loaded, with a dart, which hit me just a fraction above my right eye and fixed firmly into the bone.

I knew it was an accident, but he was so distressed about what he had done, and the possible consequences of his action, that he said "I will take you to Walworth, and let you buy anything you want, if you don't tell my Mum." Of course I agreed and we duly trotted off to town. I selected a Suwanee or sliding whistle, a cover of the Anne Shelton record "Lay down your arms and surrender to mine", a trick card game and a good wodge of pick 'n mix, now that sweet rationing had finally ended.

My main after school activity was cubs. I signed up to the local group and really enjoyed it. I loved all the practical tasks that we were given and the rituals were fun. Shaking hands with the left hand, dib dib dob dob, the special belt buckle, Akela (Old Wolf) and of course the Grand Howl, a kind of junior Freemasons. Almost immediately I fell madly in love with Brown Owl. Sadly it was not reciprocated, in fact I don't think she even noticed me. If we were ever to have a future, and live in a log cabin surrounded by wolves, I must find a way to make her notice me. I would wait for her for eternity, or at least a fortnight.

Bob a Job week came, and I saw an opportunity to shine, and get myself noticed by Brown Owl. The principle is to knock on random doors and offer to do a job for a bob, which is a shilling. I threw everything at it, and got jobs to weed the path, sweep out the garage, water the garden to mention a few. One dodgy looking guy wrote a fictitious job in my record book, and gave me two bob, without me having to do anything. My first encounter with corruption. One horrible woman made me work for three hours, cleaning out her filthy coal bunker for just a bob. I worked so hard, and put in such long hours, my Mum called a halt to it, as I was becoming exhausted.

Finally the day was here to hand in our cash and record books. Brown Owl would realise I was grown up enough to support her, in our new life in Canada, where I would protect her from brown bears, and keep her supplied with Weetabix. She called out all the participants' names followed by the sum taken.

"James, two shillings and sixpence; Simon, three shillings; Paul, three pounds, twelve shillings and six pence. Wait, yes, that's right, three pounds, twelve shillings and sixpence." I got a badge to sew on to my jumper, but not the lifelong commitment from Brown Owl I was angling for.

My spiritual life is developing now. I had passed through the childish stage, where I jumped off the end of my bed every morning, before school, in the mistaken belief that Tinker Bell would have scattered her dust, and I would be able to fly. I had spent several weeks one winter, convinced I was the second coming of Jesus Christ. Didn't tell anyone about that. Now my Dad had explained how the Tibetan people went looking for their new Dalai Lama, which they were able to recognize by a certain, but secret, birthmark. I had a birthmark on the inside of my left arm that was in the shape of a lama. That was it! I was the new, yet to be discovered, Dalai Lama that would take over shortly when the current, extremely old, one died.

Cold Water Swimming.

My academic life progressed through my early years, with me learning very little. I could hardly read or write, and may have been dyslexic, but the condition had not yet been discovered. I could read a little, by studying each word individually, but that made it impossible to string the sentence together, and extract any meaning from it. I was on, or near the bottom of the class in everything, and was generally thought of as being thick and stupid. Even when I returned to the school, a few years after I left, the Headmistress said"Of course, it was you brother John that was the intelligent one". I knew I wasn't stupid, so it didn't bother me at all.

To relieve the boredom of a school life that I found hard to engage with, I started a little business with my dyslexic friend, Ian. He was selling foreign stamps from a pyramid type company, claiming the proceeds would go towards the *Spastics Society*, and I was his representative in form 2b. We were rumbled by Mr. Johnson, and forced to donate the money we had made to the chosen charity. Since I had, however, spent some of the money, I had to start another business, selling oven-baked and vinegar pickled conkers to the booming conker trade.

St. Michael's Preparatory School was preparing me for either the *Common Entrance Exam,* so I could go on to Public School, or, the *Eleven Plu*s, so I could go on to Grammar School, which brother John had passed three years before. In fact I missed both exams as I fell ill and took to my bed. I remained off school, and mostly in bed for nearly a year, while my mother furiously looked for a diagnosis and cure. I was sick quite a bit, but I never experienced any pain. Oddly, as always, I was quite happy.

I was taken all over the place, looking for a diagnosis, including Great Ormond Street Hospital for Sick Children. This was the leading hospital for children in the country, and was famously supported by J.M.Barrie, who, in 1929, donated all rights for Peter Pan to the hospital. When asked why, he said, "At one time Peter Pan was an invalid in the hospital, and it was he that put me up to the little thing I did". Their diagnosis was that I had Salmonella. The very next day our window cleaner, who had often seen me in bed as he cleaned the windows, took it upon himself to climb in the window, and sit on the end of my bed. He talked to me about his time in the navy, the places he had been, and the strange things he had seen. He talked for over an hour, then he left.

In yet another attempt to get me out of bed and moving around, my mother asked, "Would you like to go to Cornwall to say with Auntie Val and Uncle Keith and their son Stephen?" "Er, yes!" So within a couple of days I was driven down to Cornwall by my father. After an exhausting journey we arrived late, just as the sun was setting on the hills. Wonderful to be in Looe again, staying with my favourite people.

Schools had yet to break up for the summer holidays, so Stephen would walk to school every day, and I would walk with him. At the weekend we would play, explore and spend hours beachcombing. One Saturday morning, Uncle Keith said "Would you two like to come to the Saturday morning pictures'". He owned the only cinema in Looe, so we were allowed to sit with the projectionist. Uncle Keith terrified me. He was a giant Cornish man, with a full set beard and a massive booming voice, that sounded much like the ocean crashing against the rocks.

On Sunday I went down for breakfast, to find Auntie Val having a go at Uncle Keith. "You seriously expect me to believe you were cycling along the cliff path, late at night, and two lads stopped you and stole the week's takings?". I looked at this man the size and texture of a mountain range, and thought "They must have been big lads." He had probably spent the evenings takings on gambling and drinking.

Even though it was a stormy day Stephen said "Let's walk to Looe, and let them get on with it." We took the cliff path as it was high tide, but it was hard to walk in the face of the stormy weather. As we descended to where the path runs beside the sea, a huge rogue wave appeared from nowhere, and licked Stephen off the path. His fingers were desperately scratching at the barnacle covered rock, trying by failing to gain a purchase. I immediately jumped in and managed to grab hold of his jacket, and heave with all my might, until I felt the suction give way, and I knew we were safe.

Freezing cold and soaking wet, Stephen with his bloodied fingers, we trudged home. As we stood dripping on her kitchen floor, and shivering Auntie Val said "What have you two been up to? Get in the bath straight away and no TV for you tonight." She was furious. I followed Stephen into the bath, and when I came back down the mood had completely changed. I don't know exactly what Stephen said to his mother but she came up to me and kissed me on the cheek. The little adventure was never mentioned again. The following week I returned home so I could join the rest of the family for a holiday in Spain.

Señorita.

I knew nothing of Spain, other than the national sport of torturing bulls, so I was excited to find out. The six of us left early Saturday morning, in our heavily laden estate car, boarded the ferry to Calais and started driving south. The French President, Charles de Gaulle, had started a coupon scheme, so that English tourists could buy subsidised petrol to encourage them to take their holidays in France. He soon stopped it when it became apparent that the English were using them to drive across France to Spain, just like us.

I could hardly believe what I was seeing in France. Everything was dirty, paint peeling, roofs broken, walls tumbled down, roads rutted and drains smelling. I spent many hours watching the scene unfold. A milkmaid with churns hanging from a yolk, a baker with fifty baguettes tied to the back of his bike, oxen pulling ploughs, and, every man, excepting the Gendarmes, wearing berets. I saw bomb sites, broken roads and even a church with a shell still lodged in the roof. Clearly more work to be done here.

Spain seemed even more behind and broken, but with the addition of a repressive atmosphere. Mother said "The rules are different here so make sure you behave", as we parked up to look for somewhere to get some lunch. I followed as far behind as I could mainly because of my acute embarrassment about the way my mother looked. She had a large pair of pink sunglasses, white high heel sandals and, worse of all, brightly coloured polka dot shorts. While stopping outside a restaurant, to look at the menu, a brace of Guardia Civil, they always work in pairs, confronted her. After much arm waving and gesticulation, my parents came to understand that my mother was being given an on the spot fine, for being indecently dressed in a public place. I secretly felt they were right.

We were staying in a *Rent-a-Villa,* until the drains backed up and flooded the bedroom with sewerage. The English agent moved us into one of his own places, which was new and lovely. Included in the price was the cooking, cleaning and shopping services of a beautiful señorita. I was eleven and she was eighteen, but I felt, given time, we could overcome the age difference. I went to the nearest shop, bought the largest sombrero I could find and would sit in the sun by the front door waiting for her to arrive. As she passed by me she would say something in Spanish, which I took to mean "The site of you fills me with happiness, I will wait for you for ever" but probably meant "Sit in the sun much longer and you'll get sunstroke, you silly little twit." I did get sunstroke.

Academic Success At Last.

After the summer holidays I started going to school again. My parents had done their best for me, or so they thought, and secured a place for me at Staines Grammar School. It was not really a grammar school, but in fact Mr. Parson T/A Staines Grammar School. Like my last school, it was located in a fairly large Victorian house that was badly appointed for this task. The toilet facilities were impressively poor, and rare, but probably good training for all the travelling I was planning. The only outside space was a concrete playground that was just about large enough to play British Bulldog.

The rules to play British Bulldog were simple, one boy would stand in the middle and the other boys, perhaps thirty of them, would try to get to the other wall of the playground without being picked up off the ground, for long enough to shout

"British Bulldog one two three". If that happened you would then join the boy in the middle, which made it easier to get the next one, and so on, until all the boys were in the middle, and only one left trying to fight his way through. On the occasions when I was in the middle, I would go for John, who had severe polio as a nine year old and had to wear callipers on his legs, and walk with crutches. Once I had him onside he would use his crutches to trip the next boy and we would soon gain the upper hand.

It was a strange collection of misfits really. There was a boy who could impress his classmates by taking his left eye out of its socket and putting it back, someone who spoke with an American accent, a very tall girl who smelt of urine, a Catholic boy that was allowed to miss the annual church service, and the son of someone that was divorced, whatever that meant. Every Saturday morning my Dad would bring me a cup of tea, a digestive biscuit and a copy of the comic Topper or Victor. I learnt more from looking at those comic pictures than I ever learnt at that school.

I met Pat Drinkwater at school. We became friends and one day I managed to pluck up enough nerve to ask if I could visit her. She reluctantly agreed, and on Saturday I cycled over to her house in Twickenham, which was miles away. When I arrived she wasn't in, but her mother invited me in anyway. She took to me immediately, probably because I was trained to be polite. When Pat returned home, she said she had been out with her boyfriend. I continued to visit her, every week, for months, and referred to her as my girlfriend. I soon became subsumed into her family, which comprised her younger brother and mother, the father being an absent alcoholic.

We did some things together, like going to the pictures. Of course neither of us had any money, so we financed it by bottle looking. We didn't have to go further than her back garden to find a rich cache of bottles, since her father was alcoholic. Eventually the poor off-licence owner, who probably sold Pat's father the booze in the first place, gave us the money for the pictures, on the basis we stopped bringing back any more of those filthy dirty bottles, to claim the deposit. When we got back from the pictures I overheard her mother talking to her in the kitchen. She said "He may be a bit porky now, but in a year or so, any girl would be proud to walk beside him." I didn't bother visiting much after that.

I apparently had to study hard, so I would stand a chance of passing my thirteen plus. This was a last chance saloon for pupils who had missed their eleven plus, yet may be bright enough to go on to Grammar School. My form-teacher was a Mr. C. Morden, known to all as Charlie. He used to be a priest and still wore the cloak. We all thought he had been defrocked by his church, for some sinister reason. He took an intense dislike to me, for reasons I never understood. When I received the results from my exam, he called me to stand in front of the class and announce them. Expecting me to have failed, he was not happy when I announced that I had passed, and would sit in front of an education board for an interview.

The day of the interview came, I went to the headmaster's study, to be greeted by the Headmaster, one man and three women oddly, known as *The Board*. The interview proceeded badly. When they asked if I had any hobbies, I saw a chance to redeem myself. I explained how a friend's father was a merchant seaman, and he had promised he would ask his Dad to bring me back an orang-outang, when he was next in Africa. I now know they don't come from Africa, because I have since looked it up in my Junior Encyclopedia. While I was awaiting the arrival of this orang-outang, I had been busy converting the old stable block at home to accommodate my new pet. I explained how I had planned the lighting, food preparation and sleeping area, and how I would keep a log of his behaviour. When I looked up, the Chairwoman's mouth was hanging open. I did not pass the interview.

Fun On The Water.

My time at Staines Grammar School came to an end and I was transferred to St. Paul's Secondary Modern School. A secondary Modern School was where you went if you had failed the eleven plus. It offered a focus on arithmetic and mechanical skills, such as woodwork, technical drawing, metal work, and domestic science for girls. You were not expected to continue your education after the age of 15, and, as far as I know, no one ever went on to university from st. Paul's. They were streamed as A, B, C and S. Yes, I was in the S (for special) stream and I agreed I was special. Later it was changed to special needs.

I was badly bullied at first, possibly because I talked a bit posh, but more likely because I was fat. That all changed after a few months when, through some government scheme, a community of redundant coal miners and their families were relocated to the South of England, and many of their children arrived at my school. They seemed enormous to me, kind of wedge shaped, and so much tougher, and used to scrapping. I befriended them and helped them settle in, and I was never bullied again, with one exception. I was badly beaten up outside the school gates by two girls from my school, who were on day release from a local borstal. I have no idea why.

Life continued at school with me learning almost nothing and in constant trouble, often getting beaten by the teachers with a cane or, much worse, a Plimsoll. The only bright spot was the woodworking lessons. For some unknown reason, maybe just because I asked, I was allowed to work in a separate workshop, building a Native Canadian Indian kayak. I cut out the pieces using a pattern from a sheet of marine ply and stitched them together, using soft wire. When the vessel had taken shape, I used glass fibre strips and epoxy resin to seal the seams. It was then just a case of finishing by sanding and varnishing, and of course shaping a paddle. It took a year to complete.

When it came to launch-day, I took it to the River Wey in the back of my mother's Dormobile. I paddled off and as soon as I got round the first bend, it started taking in water, probably because it needed a good soaking to swell the wood. After a few hundred yards, I was up to my waist, so I thought it prudent to pull up on this gravel beach. As it happens, there were about a dozen dustmen having their lunch by the river. They all waded out and, instead of rolling the canoe over to let the water out, they bodily lifted it onto the river bank full of water, and, in so doing, broke its back. I sold it shortly after.

Building the canoe did help me form a good relationship with my woodwork teacher, who also taught metalwork. In his spare time he had meticulously rebuilt a 1938 Velocette Kam Super Sports motorcycle. It had air rear suspension, parallel front suspension and an overhead cam-shaft. He had recorded every item he replaced, in his neat handwriting, in a large handbook with diagrams and part numbers. He told me he was forced to sell it by his landlord, and would rather sell it to someone like me, who would appreciate it, than put it in the Exchange & Mart. I bought it for five pounds.

The very next Saturday I pushed it to the common with some friends, one of whom was carrying a bottle of petrol. We put the fuel in the tank and it started straight away, and off I went across the common. After perhaps a mile, the engine faded and died. We checked for fuel and anything else we could think of as thirteen year old boys. Nothing worked, so we spent the rest of the afternoon trying to bump-start it, which also failed and was exhausting. I decided it was broken, and I would not be able to fix it, so I sold it to Jim's big brother for six pounds and a pellet air pistol. I later found out through Jim that we had failed to turn the petrol valve on.

Later that week, for some unknown reason, I was asked to play in a football match against another school. I hadn't done well at soccer, but I had the kit, so I played the match in the position of left back. Nothing much happened in the first half. I think there was a goal or two but certainly the ball never came near me. In the second half, I was suddenly confronted by a loose ball, not far from our goal. Not really knowing what to do, I ran towards it, and kicked it with all my might. It went high in the air and a sudden gust of wind caught it, causing it to sail the length of the pitch, and score the winning goal. I was the hero of the match, and even overheard one of the parents say, "Who is that boy?" Several matches later, when the sports master realised it had been a fluke, I was dropped from the team.

Red Rover.

My desire for aimless wandering started around this time. I would buy a Green Rover bus pass to get me up to London, and a Red Rover to take me around the city. I would catch the Green Line bus to some unknown suburb, from my home town of Addlestone, Surrey, where I lived with my parents and three siblings, in a wonderful six bedroom Victorian house. Sometimes, I would have a vague destination in mind, like the time I went to the Ceylon Tea Centre, for no other reason than I found the name evocative, with a sense of adventure and fascination. Oh yes, and I like tea.

I left early in the morning, and arrived at a very quiet time of day. I was greeted by the receptionist, Irangani, a tall beautiful lady, dressed in her traditional sari. She was appointed to this, her first job, by the Ceylon Tea Board in Colombo, and later progressed to the lofty position of the "Tea Queen". In the course of her job she met the Queen, the Queen Mother, Rolling Stones, Beatles and many other well known people. However, today it was wet, cold and generally miserable, and there was no one around.

When I asked her if she could explain to me how tea is grown and processed, as I was thinking of doing a project at school on the subject, her beautiful, dark brown eyes met my beautiful, dark brown eyes and I started to learn. I learnt how coffee was the first British- grown crop in the area, and it soon became among the best coffee in the world, until coffee rust disease wiped it out. Meanwhile a Scottish gentleman, by the name of James Taylor, had been sent to India by his family, to learn all there is to know about tea. This he did, and, while visiting a family friend in the regional religious capital of Kandy in Ceylon, he had a revelation. He had just visited the famous and beautiful Temple of the Tooth, where the sacred tooth of Buddha is kept, when he sat down on top of a hill, overlooking the lake, at sunset. The Indian Tea market at this time was crowded, so he wondered why not grow tea here?

This he did, and soon his plantation was growing tea, that some say, was even better than his Indian rivals. By the 1870s he was able to send his first shipment of 39 pounds, and was soon building the first tea factory in British Ceylon. One Thomas Lipton, got to hear of his enterprise, and interrupted his journey to Australia to meet James. They formed a friendship and partnership, and the Ceylon tea trade was established.

I asked Irangani how they processed tea, and she explained, "To make the best tea you must only pluck two leaves from each bud; next they are laid out to dry a little, a process we call withering, before being bruised to commence fermentation. Finally the leaves are dried, to halt the fermentation process, and we have top quality black tea. Would you like a cup?" While I drank my tea, she talked a little about her childhood, on the tea estate in the Dimbula District, known as Somerset, before some genuine, grown-up visitors arrived, and she was obliged to switch her attention. I paid my 8 pennies for the tea and left.

Feeling a little chilly, I jumped on the first bus I saw, to get warm again. It must have been going to a remote part of London, because, as the passengers got off, they were not replaced with new ones. After a while the bus was empty and the conductress started chatting to me. She started telling me about all the places that had various types of horror stories attached to them. She also said she once found a bag behind a seat with two severed fingers in them. Perhaps someone had lost two fingers in an industrial accident, and was going to hospital to have them sewn back on, and simply forgot them.

Bombed Out London.

I had always been a frequent visitor to London, due to my grandparents living in Lee Green, which is in South East London. I have fond memories of staying in this 1930s semi-detached house where I was born, and which they had owned since it was built. I remember staying there in December 1962, the year of the great smog. When I woke in the morning, and went into their bedroom, I could not see them. They had left the window slightly open, and the room had filled with smog. My Grandfather attempted, but failed to travel to his place of work at the Greenlands Docks, also known as the *Deal* docks, because it was the centre of the timber import business. Deal is a fixed stock measurement of a plank of softwood, usually imported from Scandinavia. Greenlands Docks was also central to the whaling industry and home to the ubiquitous blubber boiling houses, although that had nearly disappeared by now.

My Grandma took me to all the famous museums but my favourite by far was Horniman, established by the Horniman tea family, the largest tea traders on the planet. Both my grandparents were fans of the *World of Sport, Professional Wrestling*. On one occasion, when my Grandma could not attend, I accompanied my Grandpa. We sat in the front row where I watched Adrian Street destroy his competitor. It was a bit shocking for me, especially when someone else's grandma, sitting next to us, suddenly stood up and shouted: "Rip his arm off and hit him with the soggy end".

When the interval came, it was time for the Grand Draw. The Master of Ceremonies invited me up on the stage to help select a winner, probably because I was young, innocent-looking, and wearing school shorts. I was given a ten pound note, and asked to read off the last four serial numbers, which would be the winning ticket number. This I duly did, after which I slipped the note into my pocket, to huge applause and laughter from the audience. Even the famous wrestler, Les Kellett, also sitting in the front row, said: "Later on, when you've got some hair on your chest, come see me lad ,and I'll let you run my cafe". I had to give the ten pound note back to the MC though.

I once went for a walk in the smog and it was very strange. It had a horrible smell of sulphur that could be overwhelming, and of course, complete and utter silence. There were a few people about apparently, but I saw none. I did see a bus go past with the conductor walking in front with a large torch. It was all very exciting for a young boy, even if a little frightening. I remember returning after that walk and being filthy and in dire need of a bath. It is unsurprising that more than 500 people died in this great smog of '62.

On another occasion, my brother John and I were exploring the far corner of Grandparent's small garden, when we found an unexploded bomb. My Grandfather said he remembered three bombs falling: One hit the roof but did not go off, the second landed in the garden and blew out his french windows and the third was a mystery, until this day. He immediately called the Royal Engineers Bomb Disposal unit, known as the

Bomb Squad, and they were there within minutes. One of hundreds of shouts that year.

The Bomb Squad identified it as a Flam 250, one of 2,393 dropped on the night of 10 May 1941, during 56 consecutive nights of bombing. The Flam 250 is a 500-pound bomb, with a tremble detonator, that explodes a 3 pound *burster* charge that would spread its load of flammable oil mixture over a wide area and ignite it. Often it would not ignite, leaving a sticky and disgusting liquid, covering rooftops, streets and vehicles.

During my Red Rover jaunts around London I noticed the WW2 bomb sites. There were thousands of them after 30,000 air raids. Many remained undeveloped even in the 1960s. Some had been repurposed such as the *Bomb Site Market*, *Bomb Site Garden Party* and the *Shoreditch Bomb Site Gardens*. There were also discoveries made in these bomb sites including the Walbrook discovery of a 70 AD amphora, iron age pottery and, most spectacular of all, the 1800 year old remains of a Roman Temple, on a bomb site near Mansion House. The public were so intrigued by the discovery of this temple that thousands flocked to see it. They came in droves and caught the police by surprise, causing them to rush reinforcements to the site. There were even 60 young men dressed in Edwardian clothes, later known as *Teddy Boys*, that came to see this spectacle.

The bomb sites were unattended for so long that a culture of *Bomb Site Kids* developed. They would form clubs and secret societies, building camps in basements and lighting fires using the debris as fuel. A solid base for all kinds of mischief. Sometimes I would see so- called *Tramps*, vagrants (wandering with no fixed abode), vagabonds (vague wandering). They would be wearing broken hob-nail boots, dirty clothes and full set beard, long hair and dirty fingernails. Often they would be pushing a pram or pulling a truck, walking with hunched shoulders. They may have been ex-servicemen who had served their King and Country, only to return to find their home a bomb site, their loved ones passed away. Driven to drinking the likes of Buckfast Abbey Tonic, perhaps the cheapest and strongest wine on the market, the scourge of bombed-out London and enemy of the local councils. When funds did not permit, they would resort to drinking methylated spirits. London was a grey, miserable, mean and dirty place at the time of my wanderings but I loved it.

The Big Freeze.

In between criss-crossing London with my Red Rover, I took to writing to Embassies and High Commissions. "Dear Mr. Ambassador/High Commissioner, I love your country, and one day I would like to immigrate there, and start a sheep farm/grow tea/breed horses. Yours Faithfully, Paul Newson (Age 11). The response I got was varied. At one extreme, India sent a very nice letter, explaining they had enough people. At the other extreme, Canada sent a huge package of goodies, including a form which enabled me to apply for 160 acres of free land, providing I could farm at least 40 acres, and build a house within three years, under the Homestead Act. Touchingly, there was a handwritten pencil note at the top of the form advising me not to complete it until I was 21.

Australia was by far the best. There was a colour magazine, called *Outback*, booklets on how to breed possums, a copy of the North West Country Newspaper, covering some strange events in Birdsville and other delights. The last item I looked at was an application form, for the Assisted Passage Migration Scheme, under the Populate or Perish Policy. This allowed me to travel to Australia on one of those wonderful liners, for the princely sum of just £10. People who took up the offer were known as *Ten Pound Poms*. Again I couldn't apply until my twenty-first birthday. In all, I probably wrote to 50 Embassies and High Commissions. I believed they all replied, with the exception of Cuba and Algeria. I got bored with it in the end and decided to turn my mind to business, so that I would be able to finance some of my intended adventures.

My second attempt at business was selling second-hand bikes. I would go to the tip, and join the substantial underclass of boys and men, and search for crashed bikes and bike parts. When a dust cart arrived, the pickers would run towards the place it was being tipped, to get first dibs. I set up a workshop, in the stable block at home, and set about constructing saleable bikes. The local bike shop owner taught me how to balance a wheel by replacing and adjusting the spokes, and how to take out a cotter-pin. Even repair Sturmey Archer gears, the most reliable gear box ever made. Apparently no Sturmey Archer gear box ever broke. When one did fail during a cycle race in France, they flew an engineer out and replaced the gear box during the night. When the grateful owner wrote thanking the company, they simply replied "Sturmey Archer gear boxes don't break." Or was that Rolls Royce half shafts? Soon I had a finished product which I sold for between 2 and 5 pounds.

I knew I was lucky to have the stable block to use as a bicycle workshop. I would say I appreciate living in such a wonderful house. It has six large bedrooms, one with a pink en-suite bathroom, huge kitchen, breakfast room, sitting room leading to a *Vita-Glass* covered conservatory, lounge with french windows and, best of all, an oak-clad dining room, with a lead-lined hatch connecting to the kitchen. The outbuildings comprised a three-car garage, stable block, including the stable boy's accommodation, hayloft with a hay shoot, coach house and fruit store, all with cobble-stoned floors. There were two large, wood-framed glass-houses and a vine house with a large black grape vine, all of which are heated by an oil system and huge cast iron pipes.

The garden has a rockery, made from large lumps of multicoloured manufactured glass rocks, and planted with goldenrod and red hot pokers. There is an area of pine trees, with a pathway through it, and a fountain with a statue of a naked lady. The woods have a diverse selection of trees, and one of the last sciuridae of red squirrels. Next to the house is a large stone patio containing a fruitful fig tree and other exotics. The century-old lawn is huge with an enormous giant sequoia tree, also known as giant redwood. It really was a giant. Last week John climbed so high he appeared about the size of my thumb, much to the horror of the ever safety-conscious Aunt Alice.

It is a happy home for us four children. A place to play, learn and experiment. When we have scraps or accidents, we have our own in house first responder, in the form of Aunt Alice. Aunt Alice signed up to be a nurse in the dying days of WW1, and did some of her training in a dressing station. She spent time at the Hospital for Tropical Diseases, which was originally established as a floating hospital for seamen with leprosy and malaria. She spent time as a sister, in what used to be a workhouse, and was now called Battle Hospital, East Sussex, where I once visited her. I arrived just as the shift was about to change, and she had her staff on parade, ready for her inspection. She walked up and down and checked for clean fingernails, nylons without ladders and polished shoes amongst other things. She was there to bandage, medicate and investigate us.

I hadn't totally given up the idea of excelling in sports. Since I had done so badly at sports in school, I decided to explore opportunities outside of school. I had watched the Oxford and Cambridge boat race on television, and, since I lived quite near the Thames, decided to follow up on that idea. I looked around for a while and eventually settled on Burway Rowing Club, in Laleham-on-Thames, and simply bowled up, and asked if I could join.

It was a lovely friendly club, and, as I was by far the youngest member, they took me under their collective wing. I proved to be very poor at rowing, but good for club morale. I was given an eight, aptly named *Odds and Sods,* to cox, and soon got in the swing of it. We raced at lots of the Thames regattas, going as far as the Tideway Scullers Club and Horseferry Rowing Club in London, and some on the river Avon near Stratford. Sadly we never won anything much, but it was great fun, and I learnt how to drink and proper swear.

The pinnacle of my rowing career came during the *Head of the River* race in London. This race is performed against the clock, on a 4.25 mile course between Mortlake and Putney, on the ebb tide that has been happening almost every year since 1925. This is the same course as the Oxford and Cambridge Boat Race, held on the same day but in the opposite direction. Anything up to the limit of 420 *eights* would take part, but it was usually won by one of the big clubs like Leander based in Henley-on-Thames or London Rowing Club. The position you finished in was your starting position for the next year's race.

We rowed up from Laleham on Friday night and were guests of the Tideway Rowing Club. We were placed 232 at the starting line, and got off to a reasonable start, managing to *bump* (the signal to let us pass) two boats. We took on some water in the choppy conditions and the team began to flag. At one stage the National Provincial Bank's fourth team powered past us with the cox commenting that we were the twenty third boat they had bumped.. At least six of the team were bald or balding, which was disappointing for our young team. We made the course, an achievement in itself, and came in number 341.

I was a member of the rowing club during *The Big Freeze* of 1962-63. The club was located on the far side of the river serviced by our old Second World War pontoon to access it. This was bought from the owner of the boat yard next to the club who had made his fortune converting war time landing boats into houseboats. During the freeze we simply put two sleepers down to the ice and drove over the frozen river. The Club morphed into a drinking and poker club for the Winter. After a couple of weeks driving over the ice I went on an expedition down the frozen Thames with Jeremy. We reckoned the ice was over a foot thick, so there was no danger we could see. When we got to a weir we were able to climb over and slide down the icicles. We saw plenty of fish frozen *in situ*, including a school bream and a massive pike. The February blizzards and ten-foot snow drifts put pay to all the Winter fun.

First Love.

Things changed for me in 1962, in fact things changed for the world. Humanity held its collective breath, to see if the Soviet Union would back down from the Cuban missile crisis, or press the delete button on the human race, but this was of no interest to me; Oral Polio Vaccine was used to combat polio in the young but alas, too late for my friend John; the Beatles release *Love Me Do*, the *LED* was invented and, best of all, I met Gail.

Soon after, in 1963, the Beatles, *I wanna hold your hand,* was released, and that is exactly what we did. We held hands walking to school, for we went to the same school, although she was in the year below. We held hands and went to the Co-op Hop on a Saturday night, to see Johnny Kidd and the Pirates and other similar bands. We went to the pictures to see films like *From Russia With Love* and The Birds directed by Alfred Hitchcock, and we sat at the back holding hands. I went to her house and we sat in the living room holding hands and listening to music like *Pretty Woman* by Roy Orbison, or she came to mine and we would sit in the garden.

She was so beautiful, a true English Rose, and I had lost all my fatness. We both felt we were the Bee's Knees walking out together in Addlestone High Street. One very hot sunny Sunday afternoon I went to collect her from her house, to find her picking yellow and red roses with her mother in the garden. Her house was at the side of the family garage, and car repair workshop, and the smell of the petrol, roses, oil and summer will stay with me and forever take me back to that point in time. I was really happy.

Not long after, my parents announced they were selling our home, Audley Lodge, and moving to Looe in Cornwall. I believe my Dad's engineering consultancy business had failed, leaving them with a mountain of debt attached to the house. It didn't really sink in for some time, and it took a long time to sort out the business issues, before they could put the property on the market. It sold pretty quickly, to Findus Fish Fingers who were planning to build 46 maisonettes on the site for their employees, after this much loved house was demolished.

I saw a business opportunity here, and said to my Mother, "Since they are going to tear the house down, would you object if I had the lawn to sell?" My parents discussed it, and agreed I could. It was still the summer holidays, so I rounded up as many of my classmates as possible, especially my wedge-shaped friends from the North. I set to, marking out the turf size of 15 inches by 4 feet. Then, using a moon-shaped edge cutter, we cut to size against a plank, and cut underneath before lifting them and rolling them into the standard- looking turf rolls. We took them round to the front tarmac drive, and carefully placed them in a pile, leaving room for cars to turn round. I placed a sign by the huge wrought iron gates saying:

"100 year old weed-free turf, at an unbeatable price of 1/6d each"

They sold as fast as we could cut them, until we had turfed almost all the gardens on the new housing estate around the corner. The supplies ran out, and I at last had time to cash up and pay my crew. I had made a fortune by my standards. Enough to invest in *Henderson Far East Recovery Fund Unit Trust*. In fact it was about fourteen pounds, definitely a fortune by my standards of 9 pence pocket money per week. As it happens, 9 pence was the price of the best seats in the Saturday Morning Pictures. Some months later, in the kitchen of our next home, my parents were sitting around the table, discussing a letter from their solicitors. The buyers were apparently asking where the lawn had gone. Too late mate!

I'm Cornish Now.

Moving time had arrived and my life was again in turmoil. My emotions were pretty mixed up; I was leaving a life where I was having fun; enjoying my relationships with Gail and my other school friends, and doing no harm. On the other hand we were off to Looe! Not only that, but we were going to stay at Gradna for the winter. I knew Gradna, we had stayed there for a summer holiday, and I knew Plaidy Beach.

Gradna was a wonderful, large, white, Art Deco house built by the Wills Tobacco family in the 1930's, and sold to Lord Bath in the 1940's, as a holiday home for his family. It was planted on the cliff above Plaidy beach, with wonderful views over Looe Bay, taking in West Looe, St. George's Island, and on to Rame Head. The Mediterranean-style gardens spilled down the cliff face in a series of slate-lined cliff-top terraces, arriving at a large steel ladder, leading to a little beach. Not actually private, but not accessible to the public, except at low tide. My bedroom had a sea view, like the other five bedrooms, and its own balcony. Not all bad then?

I was missing my previous life, and I was pining for Gail. I would console myself by walking into Looe. Sometimes, at low tide, I would run along the beach. I found the best way was to keep the forward motion going, and float along with the lightest of contact with the rocks. I learnt the hard way, the safe places to make contact, like the barnacle covered rocks and the slippery rocks to be avoided. Again this forward motion thing.

It was hard to stay still, living in such an environment, with my three siblings and pregnant mother. Gradna was only a stone's throw from Stephen's home, so it wasn't long before I started to meet his friends and make friends of my own. One Sunday, Stephen said, "Would you like to come into town and see how we spend Sundays?" When we arrived in Looe, he said, "It's easy, it's called stroll'in". To do stroll'in you walk up and down Fore Street, along the Banjo, and hang out on the public benches on the prom. Every time you pass another young person, the conversation goes along the lines: "Alright? Yeah, bit boring today. What are you doing? Just strollin"

This particular Sunday there were strangers in town, and they were stroll'in too. I had never seen anyone like them. They had long hair, big beards, and jumpers down to their knees. One girl had flowing auburn hair, almost down to her waist, and another had a guitar slung on her back. Most had sleeping bags, one had an intricately carved walking stick. There was even a small dog, and a girl smoking a pipe. Who were these people? Where were they from, and where were they going?

Stephen told me they identified as Beatniks. A social movement with its roots in 1950's America, that believed in a non-materialistic lifestyle, that was influenced by the likes of Jack Kerouac's book, *On the Road.* Some say the word Beatnik comes from beaten-down or downtrodden, others that it relates to beatitude, spiritual. When I grow up, I want to be one of them.

Before we left town that day, we went to the Fishermen Pub for a half of cider shandy. I know, I was only fifteen, but underage drinking and smoking was widespread, and generally accepted down here. I think it was because there was so little for young people to do, that it was thought that at least the *town* could keep an eye on their young in the pub.

I was surprised to see some of the Beatniks in the pub, one leaning against the bar. His accent sounded like one of my wedge shaped miner friends from school, so I'm thinking he is probably from the Nottingham area. I said: "I saw you in town earlier. Where are you from?" He said, "I was born in Derby, but I left home to go on a long walk." I said, "Did you hitch down?" He said, "No, I walk everywhere. I've been walking for three years." Did I still want to be like them? Probably, but I will think about it.

Before long I became integrated into the local set, although I was probably the youngest. This was Cornwall in the winter, so it means parties every Saturday night. I went to parties in peoples houses, a party in a fisherman's workshop, parties in barns and village halls. It was such good fun, I loved it. It wasn't very long before I met a local girl called Mary. After a few meetings in the pub, and a couple of parties, she said, "Would you like to come to my place on Sunday, and stay for tea?"

She lived some way out of town, so I hitch-hiked, and walked the last couple of miles. When I arrived at her house, I was greeted by Mary and her Mum, a tiny Chinese lady, with a reasonable command of English. I was introduced to her Dad, a giant Scottish man, who vigorously pumped my hand. They were lovely people, so it didn't take long for me to start getting on well. Meeting new, big people like this never phased me. I seemed to have a lot of self-belief and self-confidence, for no apparent reason.

I asked her Dad, "What do you do on your farm?" He said, "We run an egg farm, and all our product goes to the Egg Marketing Board. Would you like to look around?" He showed me from the start to the end of the process, with me constantly asking questions. He was proud of his cutting-edge technology. I learnt how he chooses the feed from a colour chart, so the yolk and shell colour are exactly right for his market. I learnt how the battery hen sheds were heated and lighted all the time, and how the eggs rolled onto a conveyor belt, one of which was jammed. As he bent down to fix it, I stole my first kiss from Mary, except it was her idea, so it wasn't really stealing, was it?

Life had become settled in Looe, and I was again having lots of fun. My Dad was commuting to Exeter, with Uncle Keith, and my mother was in the last three months of pregnancy. My Dad, as a self-identified technocrat, really was not suited to selling insurance on commission, and probably wasn't making enough money to support us lot. The search for a new home and a school for me, was not going well either. On Saturday morning, he said, "I've been speaking to some old colleagues, and I have been offered an engineering job in Slough." I filled in the blanks myself, "So we will be moving to near Slough".

Moving time came, and I went with my local friends for a last night out. We got a bit drunk in the Bullers Pub, and moved on to the Banjo, when the pub shut. It was high tide, so the day-fishing boats could return with their catch, ready for the early morning auction. One of my crowd knew one of the young fishermen, and a dialogue developed. He said, "Ahoy, *bucket-head*, still not caught anything?" Another said, "Ask *fin-slayer* to give you a hand," referring to the booming shark fishing business, which was for tourists, and not proper fishing.

Drawing parallel, was a boat called *Our Girls,* owned and operated by Jack and his wife, known as *Betty Fats*. Jack stood on the deck with a large fish in his hand, took aim, and hurled it with all his, not inconsiderable, might. It flew through the air, and smacked me in the face with such force, it knocked me off my feet. What a shot! Everybody laughed, including myself, after I had removed the fish scales from my eyes, nose and mouth. So, for now, my life in Looe ended.

Runaways.

I spent a few weeks staying in a hotel in Maidenhead, while my Dad took up his employment in Slough. I attended Slough College of Further Education, in a last ditch attempt at formal education. Of course it didn't work out well, and it didn't last, but I did make some new friends. One was a Sikh named Amanpreet, which means one who loves peace. He was the first person I had ever spoken to, let alone befriended, that was not from a white Caucasian background. His father was a businessman, and he gave his son a Ford Zephyr, to help him attend college. We went everywhere in his car, and had so much fun.

College just fizzled out, and I stopped going altogether after a few weeks. Meanwhile, my Dad had become firmly ensconced in his mechanical engineering consultancy job in Slough, and my Mum was getting close to giving birth. It didn't diminish her energy levels though, and in no time, she had located a rental house in the middle of the Oxfordshire countryside, two miles from the lovely village of Checkendon. We moved in and we were together as a family again.

The house was a lovely converted barn, owned by Colonel Wilkinson and his wife. They lived in the main house by themselves, and Mrs Wilkinson ran a small chicken farm as a hobby business. It was a beautiful location and a wonderful house to live in, but as a 15 year old, I felt trapped. Even when I did manage to escape, by way of walking four miles to the nearest road, where would I go? Wallingford, Reading, Henley-on-Thames? I knew no one in any of those places, so I just took potluck.

I was missing Mary and I was missing my life in Looe. I was in contact with Mary, and one day she phoned me and said "Would you like to come down and stay with me for a couple of weeks?" I cleared it with my parents, who probably made the mandatory phone call to Mary's parents, and I was packed and on my way. This was my first big hitch-hike that I had done alone.

After the four mile walk to the road, I got a lift from a rough looking truck, driven by a rough looking driver. After a few minutes of him talking, in an accent that I could hardly understand, he reached across and tried to grab at my crotch area, saying something like, "Oh 'ere nipper I bet you got a 'ard 'on." "What's a hard-iron?" I replied. "You know, a 'ard 'on." he repeated. "I don't know what a hard iron is." This went on for a few more miles, with him repeatedly trying to grab my crotch, when he was forced to stop at some traffic lights and I was able to make my escape.

A couple of lifts took me to the A303, where a nice new-looking car stopped and offered me a lift, right the way to Plymouth. When I asked him what he did for a living, expecting him to say a dog food travelling salesman, or something like that. He said "I work for a strip tease club in London. My job is to travel around the country, interview and assess the bodies of young women who have responded to our advert for strippers." Gosh it is a big wide world I had gone out into.

I arrived at Mary's, and settled into my room in the west wing of the house. I made myself useful over the next couple of days, washing up, collecting eggs and anything else they would let me help with. After a couple of days we decided to go into town for the afternoon. Mary had been given a new Lambretta scooter for her sixteenth birthday, and had just started to learn to drive it. As a learner, she was only allowed to take a passenger if they had a full motorbike licence. I lied, and we drove off to town, with me on the back.

Barely three miles from her home, there is a long slow hill and Mary just could not get up it without stalling, so I took over. Halfway up the hill we were pulled over by a motorcycle policeman, who asked to see Mary's and my driving licence. Mary duly produced her licence, and I was left having to do some fast creative thinking, also known as winging it. I said, "I do not have a licence. I was walking up the hill and I saw this person, whom I have never seen before in my life, struggling to drive her scooter up the hill. Since my Dad owned a motorcycle shop, and he had taught me to drive on the local disused aerodrome, I thought it right that I should help her." "Well" he said, "You were breaking the law, but you did the gentlemanly thing, so I will just take your names and addresses and let it pass for now".

It seemed we had gotten away with it, but I was worried that he had taken our names and addresses. We drove straight home, taking as many minor roads, tracks and bridleways as possible and pretended nothing had happened. We had just finished eating supper when there was a knock on the door, which Mary's Dad answered. I could hear the low rumble of serious, grown up voices and then the visitor was invited in, at which point I caught a glimpse of his uniform and legged it upstairs to hide.

I could clearly hear the conversation, as the policeman related how this young gentleman had rescued his daughter, and how he thought she should have some lessons before going on the road again. I had crossed a line and broken the law and got away with it. After he had left her Dad said "I am wondering if I should ask you to leave". I did the decent thing and left early the next morning. That morning was the last time I ever saw Mary.

It seemed a pointless waste, and difficult to explain, if I went home now. I had my cover for the next two weeks so I might as well turn it into an adventure. I decided to head down into deepest Cornwall, to places I had heard about and sounded exciting, say Newquay, for example.

When I arrived in Newquay, it looked like I had made a good choice. The sea was that deep, deep blue, apparently caused by the special light on the North Coast, the sand was golden and clean and there were lots of happy people. Lining a wall were a dozen or so Beatniks. I didn't recognize any of the faces, but I did recognize the beautiful hand carved walking stick that one of them carried. I had seen that stick before in Looe.

There seemed to be a much younger crowd sitting on the beach, and generally hanging about. They were dressed differently, and had longer hair. I was soon talking to them and watching with great interest, but not participating, in their joint smoking. As the sun was setting, we collected driftwood and lit a fire. Someone took out a guitar and started singing a song about the colour of his true love's hair in the morning. I met Linda.

Linda was a little older than I, like most people I hung out with. She was rather beautiful and had an easygoing way about her. She was born and bred on a dairy farm just outside St. Austell, and had never left Cornwall. She said, "I got so fed up telling people, *I'm trying to connect you,* that I decided to take a week off from my job at St. Austell Telephone Exchange, and explore the world." I knew of a big party this weekend in Walton-on-Thames, through contact I still had with an old school mate. I said "Would you like to come up-country with me to a party. We can hitch-hike and be there in good time?" She said, "Why not?"

After a pretty unpleasant night, sleeping on the beach, in my old blanket sleeping bag I had bought off one of the Beatniks, we were up at the crack of dawn and on the road heading up-country. It was so much easier for a boy and girl to hitch a lift, that we were there, just about as quickly as if we had driven directly. Linda was trying to look cool, but I could detect her excitement at seeing life outside of Cornwall.

The party was great. I met up with a couple of old mates, we all got a bit drunk, and had a ball. When it came to going home-time, Linda and I went off to find somewhere to sleep the night. I remembered, from my rowing days, that the Walton Regatta was on this week so we headed off Thames-side. By now it was the early hours and we were exhausted, so we took the first opportunity to bed down, which took the form of the tent where the rowing eights were stored for the night. We both got into the slightly damp sleeping bag, cuddled up and almost immediately fell asleep.

Sometime later we were woken by a bright torch in our faces, and a voice saying, "Well well, look what I've found here." The eights are very valuable crafts and there were perhaps twenty in this tent, so of course the tent would be patrolled by the police. We saw ourselves as being on a fairly innocent adventure, but the police would have seen us as two children sleeping rough. We were taken to the police station and interviewed separately. I was allowed to leave on the basis that I would go straight home to Checkendon, but Linda was kept until arrangement could be made, with St. Austell police, to have her returned to her family.

I felt awful. I could only imagine how it must have been for her parents. They must have been so anxious that their child had gone missing, then to find out she had been abducted by an unknown man. I strolled up and down the river bank thinking and wondering what to do, when I thought, "I know, I will go and see Linda's parents and explain it to them. I would set off immediately and travel through the night." The police had kindly allowed us to swap addresses before we were separated.

The last bit of the journey took a long time, so I didn't arrive at the farm until around eleven on Sunday morning. I knocked at the door, which was answered by a man in overalls, smelling of cows. I said, "I am the boy who took Linda to a party in Walton." He was so angry he couldn't say a word, but just called his wife. She said, "Do you know how worried we've been? We thought something horrible may have happened to her. All the local community has been out searching." I said "Sorry". What else could I say? She said, "Well you've come all this way, you better come in."

She gave me a cup of coffee and a biscuit, and after a while the Dad had calmed down enough to give me a right royal bollocking, which I probably deserved. I took it all on the chin, and was as polite as I knew how. I believed my well-being depended on my manners. After a while it all quieted down, and she said, "You're here now, would you like some lunch?" I said, "Yes please. Can I give you a hand in the kitchen?"

The Sunday roast that came out of her kitchen, that Sunday lunch time was nothing short of magnificent. I tucked in and cleaned my plate. She said, "Would you like some more?" I said, "Yes please." I refilled my plate. She said, "I like to see a boy with a good appetite." I helped her with the washing up, and helped the Dad with feeding the pigs. Through a combination of good manners, clean looks and, most important of all, an enormous appetite, I had won them over.

Had I not done all this, it would have been horrible for them. To not know what happened and with whom, would have been disturbing for a long time. Without knowing it at the time, I had probably done one of the kindest things I had ever done in my life, so far. As for Linda, well she had had her adventure, and would probably not be going up-country again any time soon. We kissed goodbye, and I never saw or heard of her again.

Working.

Life was seriously dull in Checkendon. It was a lovely place, but there really was nothing to do. I had been hitching to Reading from time to time, only to sit in a cafe by myself, and hitchhike home again. I had more success in Henley, where I first met Hugh. I was therefore delighted when my parents announced we were moving to Henley-on-Thames.

I decided to look for a job. In no time at all, I had found a job, as an assistant drays-man for Brakspears Brewery in New Street, which of course was the oldest street in Henley-on-Thames. The contract was for 45 hours a week, including Saturday morning, for which I would be paid £4/7/6d, and as much as I could drink from the barrel of bitter and barrel of mild, located in the staff canteen. Tea and coffee were not available.

The job involved ridin' with Old Ned, who had been on *locals* since the war. In other words helping him deliver to the 52 pubs in the Henley-on-Thames town area. Often it was necessary to wake up the publican, for the *earlies*, and drop off his requirements. This involved dropping the barrel onto a sack of hops and rolling it into his cellar. I could manage the 36 gallon barrel, but the 54 gallon hogshead required two of us. Old Ned would help with the hogshead, and leave me to do the barrels, firkins – Ned claimed he named it after one dropped on his foot -- and pins while he sat at the bar, to receive his tip of a pint or two. I counted one day, he was up to 27 pints. A bit unsteady on his feet, but still able to slump behind the wheel and drive the truck around.

After a few weeks I was developing a bit of a taste for early morning pints. Anyway, the work was hard, so I decided to move on up and try my hand at something else. I selected The Catherine Wheel as my next employer, and went for an interview. The manager had an eye for *bright young things,* and gave me a job on the spot, operating the deep fat fryer, churning out vast amounts of part-cooked chips for their eight restaurant bars. I excelled at the task so the job was expanded to include the potato peeling and chipping machine.

Several tons of chips later, I asked the manager for a promotion to the job of wine waiter, and was given it. I had a good knowledge of beer by now but no knowledge of wine, so I had to wing it. Fortunately, most of the customers had no knowledge of wine either. I was earning more money now and getting tips, on top of my wage. I could have gone on from there, I could have worked my way up to manager, become something in catering. I could have got married, bought a house and had a good life in Henley-on-Thames. It didn't happen, because of what I call black Thursday.

I served this particular table with a bottle of wine, which was fine, except I managed to allow a lump of cork to get into the alpha male's glass. When he called me over to tell me of this appalling event, I said, "Sorry sir," and proceeded to plunge my hand in his glass to capture the piece of cork. He called the manager over, who gave me a blasting.

Shortly afterwards, I served another table of apparently important people. I was very careful to avoid the previous mishap and managed a successful pour. The gentleman at the head of the table called me over, and said, "I have checked against the menu, and noticed you have charged me for three schooners of sherry instead of two. You have also added up the total wrongly." I said, "I may have inadvertently charged you for an additional schooner of sherry, but it has certainly been calculated correctly Sir." Unfortunately, he was The Right Honourable Roy Jenkins, the current Chancellor of the Exchequer. Time to move on.

I thought the building trade may be a way to earn good money, so I could follow up on my dreams, and go to East Africa, wherever that is. There was quite a large site, up Gravel Hill, so I went looking for a job. I was offered the job as tea boy. My job was to keep the tea hut clean, place bets on horses for the builders, go to the cafe and buy their bacon sandwiches and get any shopping required from the town. My boss said, "Nip into the hardware store and pick up a box of rubber tin tacks, and a dozen large skyhooks". Off I duly trotted, but when I got to the shop, and placed my order at the counter, the shop assistant said, "The rubber tin tacks won't be in until Tuesday. What size skyhooks do you want, 14 or 18 inch?"

Most of the notorious local bad boys seemed to work here. I recognized Mick, Dan and Phil from drinking in the Catherine Wheel. They were extremely strong and huge. They were all mates from the military. They did their National Service, then signed up for a stint in the Heavy Artillery, which is where their nickname of *The Heavy Brigade* came from. They were marginals, and famously turned up at the Catherine Wheel, wearing white coats. They politely asked the guests to move, moved all the furniture to one side, and rolled up the large, valuable rug, loaded it onto their pickup and took it away. It was days before management noticed it had been stolen.

After many trips to Jock's Box Cafe to buy their bacon sandwiches, I spotted a business opportunity. I checked with my boss first and made a modest investment in a camping stove, some pots and pans. I was soon turning out a range of breakfasts and lunches at a significant discount on Jock's Box. I even started experimenting with home made soups, which I found to be highly profitable. Everything I served was either in tea mugs or on old newspapers, which was not very hygienic. I had to stop using old newspapers, when one egg sandwich I served Mick had the football results printed on the underside.

The boss's office was located, up some steel steps, in the middle of the site. Rather like a watch tower in a prisoner-of-war camp, it gave him eyes on the whole site. One morning, a large expensive looking black car turned up. Three besuited gents got out and proceeded to the office. After a while, the boss leaned out of his office and shouted, "Titch", as he was inclined to do when he needed something. I trotted up, and took his order for tea, for four. I got out the special cups and saucers, and teapot, reserved for visiting dignitaries, and made a brew, with Rich Tea biscuits on the side, and took it up to them.

As it happens we had been having some issues with the temporary water supply. We think some derv fuel had contaminated the water, which caused the tea not to infuse correctly. After the visitors had left, the boss shouted for me again. When I climbed the steps, thinking I was just going to collect the used tray, he said "Titch that tea didn't have the strength to crawl up the ******* spout. You're fired." I was okay with that.

Life In A Bubble.

I was now sixteen, old enough to ride a motorbike under 250cc. When I asked permission to buy one, my Mum said, "Ask Aunt Alice". I did, and she said, "I was working as a sister in Accident and Emergency, during the age of the *Ton-up Boys,* and have seen so many young men lose their legs, I forbid you to buy a motorbike. You can buy a scooter though, at least your legs might be around longer."

Aunt Alice was often around, and we were all happy with that. She was always there to patch us up, put ointment on our infections, kill our parasites and answer all our medical questions like: "Will chewing gum stop me feeling hungry?" or "What's pus made from?" or "Will my legs always be bandy?" We always listened and she was always right, so I listened this time, and decided to look for a scooter.

I found a scooter that fit my budget called a Diana. It was manufactured by a German company called Durkopp, who were really industrial sewing machine manufacturers, turning their hand to another product. It was old, failing and very unfashionable, which is exactly why I could afford it. Within a week of buying it there was an issue with the front wheel bearings and I was obliged to take it to a specialist.

As there was only a slim chance of making it to the repair shop, without breaking down, Mum kindly agreed to follow me in her car. Passing through one of the villages, the front wheel seized and I skidded into a wall. I went flying over it, doing a double-flip on the way, and landed on a mossy pile in the graveyard, between two graves. I sat up, completely unhurt. My poor Mum must have thought: "My sons' dead; he's alive but a vegetable; he's completely unhurt. Okay, carry on."

Shortly after this episode, Mum said, "Your father and I have decided it will be safer if we buy you both a new *Lambretta*." Wow! They had never done anything like that before. Shame it wasn't a *Vesta* though, much more on trend. First stop was to the *Army Surplus* store to buy a *M51 Fishtail Parka,* with a detachable fibreglass lining and wolverine-fur collar, as issued to the US Army. Next I cut the tail off my *Davy Crocket* hat, which for some reason, I still had laying around, and tied it to the rear aerial. I was a *Mod*.

I didn't take to it. It seemed to mostly involve popping pills, like *Bust Aid*; an amphetamine- type drug for slimming and bust reduction, available over the counter in Spain; or *Drinamyl* tablets, known as *Purple Hearts*, another stimulant drug. Other requirements were, listening to *I Can't Explain* by the *Who*, and going to the South Coast to indulge in a mass punch-up with the *Rockers* on Bank Holidays. *Rockers* were about the same as *Mods* but riding motorbikes, wearing leather jackets and lots of grease. Not for me, so I rebelled against being a rebel Mod.

Now living in Henley, and equipped with my scooter, life was opening up for me. I was able to try different types of employment, including customer service in a coach office, petrol pump attendant, washing up in a pub, hod carrier, shop assistant in a cycle spare parts counter, and others. At this time it was possible to quit a job on a Friday evening, and start a new one on Monday morning, pretty much without fail. We all did that often. I had made a lot of friends in the area, and I was happy and optimistic about the future.

My next job was working with a road-resurfacing contractor. My job was to stand on the board at the back of the tar-laying tanker, and open or close the valves to make the tar-strip wider or narrower, depending on the road width. This is where I first met Dave. He was not long back from conscription into the Army. He had served in British Malaya, and was permanently scarred by the experience of shooting a woman dead in an ambush, only to find out she was carrying firewood and not arms. I had just missed conscription by about five years.

Dave's job was to drive this huge road-roller, after the gravel truck had done its job. On this particular day, we were working on a small rural lane, when he appeared on my tar board, apparently for a chat. I asked him who was driving his road roller, and he said, "Me! I put the throttle on low and set the steering." After a few seconds, he ran back to it and rescued the situation, before disaster ensued, in the form of a large oak tree, a few yards in front. He was crazy, but then he had tattoos on his arms. At the time if you had a tattoo, you were either a merchant seaman or a bit mad.

I had had enough of this low-paid casual-labour type work. Time to get a serious career under my belt. I sent out many job applications, a bit like the letters to the Embassies in my early years. Job-application forms and offers of interviews started to trickle in. I invested £4/7/6d on a sharp Italian suit, and went to a couple of interviews, where the potential employer had offered to pay the travel expenses. At one interview, the person interviewing me slapped a mass of tangled wires, and components on the desk and said, "Do you know what this is laddie?" I said "Is it a part of a computer?" He simply shook my hand and said, "Safe journey home young man."

Finally I was offered a job as a chartist, whatever that was. No amount of research helped me ascertain what my future career might look like. I was to start at the beginning of the month, in about three weeks time. Since it was a considerable distance from home, and I would be wearing a suit daily, it did not seem viable to travel there by scooter. I was only sixteen but I was able to drive a three-wheeler, so I sold my *Lambretta* and set about finding a suitable vehicle.

I bought a *Messerschmitt* three-wheeler, also known as a *Bubble Car*. The *Messerschmitt Aircraft Factory* in Germany was banned from making planes, for obvious reasons. The company turned its skills, production capacity, design expertise, and mountain of spare aircraft parts, to making the *Bubble Car*. Fend Flitzer, famous for his invalid carriage design, was appointed chief designer. The result was a wonderful example of over-engineering.

The bubble was made of acrylic, and, or so the salesman said, was bullet proof. Lifting the bubble was the way to enter the vehicle. The body-work was designed by some of the best aircraft designers in the world, and incorporated an aircraft-style fuselage, with low air-drag. As if that matters at 35mph. The engine was a 175cc, forced air cooled, *Fichtel & Sachs,* single cylinder, two-stroke job, with a four-speed gearbox. To gain reverse it was necessary to stop the engine, push the ignition key in further, and restart. This allowed you to use all four gears in reverse. The shock absorbers were hydraulic and most effective. All that, for £34.

The reality was something different. The reverse-gear system was prone to breaking, meaning it was necessary to get out and push the car backwards. There was no windscreen wiper, fuel gauge or heater. The driver's seating was incredibly cramped, like the cockpit of a fighter plane, and the controls were modified aircraft controls, including a joy stick of sorts to steer it. Worst of all the engine was very unreliable, and prone to frequent breakdowns, which your average car mechanic was not able to repair. Let's hope it's up to the job.

On my first day at my new job, my role was explained, and I was able to unravel the title of *chartist*. I was working for a market survey company, helping to produce their weekly reports, for their multinational customers. My job was to plot that particular week's sales, by extending a thick black graph-line on a plastic sheet, which would then be transferred to a stencil and printed in quantity. Not the most demanding thing I have ever done.

The main problem with the job was the journey. At an average speed of 32 mph, and numerous breakdowns, it took forever to get to work, and get home again. Something had to change. I thought I would try staying in the town, but I was unable to find any lodgings at a reasonable price. I thought I would see if I could actually sleep at work. One evening I said good night to my co-workers, and slipped back past them, claiming I had forgotten my keys, then hid in the toilets until they had all left. It worked, so I made a habit of it.

The evenings were long and boring. I would just wander around the offices and into the sister company, where they repaired electronic equipment of some sort. Fiddling with knobs and trying to start up the pieces of equipment, especially the ones that looked like TVs, eating my sandwiches and having the occasional shower. All done in darkness of course. This lasted for a few weeks, until the receptionist started to take note of my movements. She thought it strange that, suddenly, I was always the first into work. My line manager called me in and said, "You're a nice lad but you're fired."

I had saved quite a bit of money by now. Nearly enough to have a stab at going to East Africa. I sold my *Messerschmitt* to an individual, who was about to set out on the driving adventure of his life, but didn't yet know it. I now had enough money. The Labour Party, under Harold Wilson, had set a limit on the amount of funds it was possible to take out of the country. The limit was £50 in traveller cheques, and £15 in cash, so having any more was pointless. I talked to Hugh down the pub that night, and we agreed to set off next week.

When I announced to my mother, I was going to Africa, she said, "Oh no you're not, you're only seventeen". I said, "I am," and left it at that. It was never mentioned again. About three days later she was at her sewing machine, making a special pouch for my money and passport. My parents were probably up late into the night, discussing what could be done with me. I knew nothing of that, and wouldn't have cared anyway. So Hugh and I left Henley-on-Thames on a grey March morning.

On The Road.

Hitch-hiking was a success on our journey through France, but ground to a halt in dusty old Spain. From there on we took the train, which was not what we had planned, so the budget was out the window straight away. No matter how much I commuted on a steam train to my private school in Staines, I was in no way prepared for the experience of riding Spanish trains. As the train steamed into the station, something like a riot broke out. People were climbing in windows, fighting to get on, even trampling nuns, just to get a seat. Not expecting it, we had no chance of finding our own seats. Since the journey was going to take days, we decided to camp in the toilet, with our bread, cheese, squashed tomatoes and ample amounts of wine, stored in some kind of strange animal-bladder thing, that later evolved into tourist tat.

The train thundered, well actually plodded, through the plains of central Spain. We were quite comfortable, in what you could call the suite part of an en-suite. We had food, rolling tobacco, wine, space for sleeping and of course a toilet and running water. The only annoying thing was the increasingly desperate knocking on the door.

We got off the train and again took to the road. The final lift of the day involved coming down the mountains, through the clouds, into the city of Malaga. A beautiful city, possibly the most ancient in Europe, and one of the oldest continually inhabited cities in the world, with lovely old buildings. But something had gone wrong in Spain! There was a kind of shanty town on the beach, which was littered with several dead dogs, one of which was just a skeleton. Dog fighting, starvation and of course no tide to clean the beach twice a day.

We went into a bar to eat and drink, at remarkably cheap prices. It was a warm, lively place with the sounds of happy people. There was a large bowl of mussels on the bar. Occasionally one would leave its shell and slither over the side of the bowl, and start to travel up the bar. Every time this happened, one of the bar staff would swallow it. Kind of a bonus I guess?. At what point in the process did the mussel die?

Suddenly a deathly silence fell over the place, as a pair, always a pair, of Guardia Civil entered the bar with their funny shaped *tricornio* hats. Apparently, during Napoleon's invasion of Spain, the local police resisted, and were often shot by a firing squad. They refused to take off their police hats, and, when they had their noses pressed to their execution wall, their hats were forced into that odd shape. I wasn't afraid, but the fear in the room was palpable. This was a different country. I was really learning stuff now. I knew it was a better education for me than university. Not just sour grapes, because I was in the "S" stream at school, and therefore had no chance of further education anyway. When I asked what the "S" stood for, I was told that I was special. I always thought I was a bit special because my Mum had told me so. Much later they devised the term *Special-needs*. I do have special needs but doesn't everyone?

After a few days sleeping on the beach, we moved down to Torremolinos. Wandering around the beachfront, there seems to be a choice of a German, English or American bar. We chose the American bar, which was a good choice, since it was kicking. People playing guitar, smoking pot, gambling with their "hot potatoes' or, as we call them, Pesetas. We had a great night hanging out with the draft dodgers and listening to their tales of how they tried to avoid the draft. Some talked of various medications that changed the colour of their skin to yellow or orange, or gave them nasty looking rashes. Some pretended to be deaf, blind or psychopaths. Just simply being a homosexual would do it. If all of these failed they just fled, rather than go to an unknown country, and kill fellow humans for reasons they did not understand. I don't blame them.

We took to the road again, and arrived in a small town called La Linea. From here it was just a walk to Gibraltar. The border had not yet closed, but there was talk of it closing. What a strange contrast to cross from the dusty, repressive confusion of Franco's Spain, to the red telephone boxes, clean streets and bobbies of Gibraltar. The police were a little shorter, fatter, and somewhat Spanish looking, but their uniforms looked identical. Even the drains smelt good. There were some differences, like the street signs, threatening a fine of 1/3d for spitting in public, sub-tropical plants, and the weather of course.

Within minutes we saw a sign: *Smokey Joe's full house for half a crown*. It felt like home. Well, perhaps, more like the Busy Bee on the A1 on a Saturday night. We were determined that this man, probably Joe, or could be Smokey, was not going to make a profit out of us. We ate until we could eat no more, and bedded down for a night's sleep, on this huge rock, a few feet above the beach. It must have faced East, because there was the most wonderful sunrise over the sea in the morning. Was the tide in or out? Does it have the tide of the Atlantic or the Mediterranean? Does anyone know the answer? Does it matter anyway?

After a few days, we were stopped in the street by an English gentleman, who looked and spoke, remarkably like I imagine Bertie Wooster would have looked and spoken. He said he had a proposition for us. Would we like to visit his yacht this evening to discuss it over supper? It was a luxury ten-birth vessel, nearly full with his furniture. Apparently, he was on his way to Italy, with his much younger wife and small child, to build some kind of holiday business there. The proposition, discussed over a wonderful fish supper, was to crew his yacht, to his destination, in the Gulf of Naples. We were intending to go to Morocco, but we changed our minds, and decided to go with the flow, mainly because he and his wife were so charming and friendly, and the food was so good, and we didn't have anywhere to stay that night anyway.

A Life At Sea.

We were allocated our cabin, and set sail early the next morning. Almost immediately the mood changed. He stopped being nice, and made us practise ridiculous rope throwing exercises. The food deteriorated to slops. We had to take the helm, four hours on, and four hours off. During one of my night shifts, I lashed the wheel to the approximate heading, and went to the bar, in the lounge, to hit the whiskey, for the second and last time in my life. I was jolted out of my drunken stupor, as the boat turned into the waves, and was thrown madly about, causing Mrs. Mercer's infant to roll off his or her, (I never found out which), bunk and crash to the floor. I managed to rest the boat so it was again at right angles to the waves, and on an even keel. Several hours later, it became obvious that we were 180 degrees off course.

After many days and nights of this relentless shift system, we arrived in Nice. By that time, the lack of sleep and food, and Mr. Mercer's relentless bullying, had taken its toll. I had developed an intense dislike of the man, influenced in part by the way he bullied and abused his younger, and much more agreeable wife. The hours of training clicked into play. Hugh stood in the stern and I stood in the bows, both of us clutching our coiled ropes. In fact, since we were touching the harbour I had only to throw my rope some eighteen inches, so all that rope throwing training was a complete waste of time.

We were allowed off the boat, to wander around the harbour, and told to be back by dark. Mr. Mercer had taken our passports for safe keeping, which he said was normal on-board practice. We made our way to the Black Cat Bar, and got horrendously drunk, on an unknown green French spirit. It was here, leaning against the bar, that I hatched my plot. The plan was simple: I would slip back to the boat, while the Mercers were still stocking up on supplies, retrieve our passports and liberate the pay we were due, from the large block of new 1000 lira notes, which he kept in a drawer under the bar. Hugh and I would then return to the boat together, after we were sure they were in bed. We would pack and leave at first light when the gate was opened, but before the customs arrived.

All went to plan. I found the passports and block of notes, and was tempted to take it all, but decided that I would only take what was due. We managed to get past the security guard by explaining, *"Mon patron est formidable."* and we were away. The perfect crime? *Non*. I had dropped a postcard down the side of my bunk. It had been written and addressed to Aunt Alice. Mr. Mercer had simply written to Aunt Alice, said I had left some of my things behind, so could he have my address. He had my address, I had his money, I was a fugitive, I was off to Africa.

After a 18 hour train trip, we were standing in Bologna railway station. We knew we had to go south to ever reach Africa. We were in a hurry to get there, and Sicily seemed the most southerly point, and Palermo looked useful. I found a railway employee who spoke English, and asked him when the last train to Palermo leaves. "Maybe never," was his reply. I knew *Express* was quicker than *Local*, but was *Rapido* quicker than *Express*? I said "What do you reckon Hugh?" He replied, "Let's take no chances, and go for the *Super Rapido Express* to Rome." In no time we were passing The Leaning Tower of Pisa. I was surprised, and would probably be surprised if I ever see it again. I never really understood why the train went down that side of Italy though.

The next leg of the journey took us to *Roma*. Particularly memorable, for a chance meeting with a very important English Catholic priest, on a mission to Rome. I knew he was important, because of the purple in his clothing, and the number of cochineal beetles that must have gone into dyeing them. At the time I was smoking a local brand of cigarettes, called *Africa*, with a picture on the packet of a bare breasted black woman with an elongated neck carrying a pot on her head.

I already had the *Spanish boots of Spanish leather,* and the rolled up, blanket-type sleeping bag, as used in the American Civil War at Gettysburg so the cigarettes seemed to fit the image. When one is seventeen years old one has to create an image from scratch, unless you see one that fits and borrow it. Not just a case of *finding* yourself, I wanted to be different, there again so did most other people I knew.

Some things worked, others didn't. The sleeping bag was eventually abandoned, for being far too heavy, especially when wet, not waterproof, not warm, so completely useless. A shame considering how good it looked. The cigarettes were not available anywhere else on the planet, but the boots remained with me. In fact, I now look back at Rome as the start of a beautiful relationship with those boots.

The English man sitting opposite me, in the black and purple gowns, said, "Is that picture of a black lady, with the marvellous pair of breasts, from Africa?" Without hesitation, I gave the slightly strange reply of yes. I realise now this was his way of counteracting his flowing black and purple gowns, and communicating with a young person. It worked, and we had one of those few conversations that you remember all your life. Can't remember what it was about though.

Some hours later the train pulled into Rome, where my new-found friend, and first spiritual guru, was met by a welcoming party. I had loads more things I wanted to ask him, but he was going now, trains are like that. I believe he could have answered some questions, that could take me a further half a lifetime to find out. His parting words were, "Keep on searching until......" At that point one of those platform carts, carrying empty bottles, rattled past.

With God on my side, and some hours to kill, we went on a mission to find a spaghetti house. Price conscious, we took to the back streets. We passed world-class buildings with as much awareness as, well, just about any traveller, prior to Gibbon's visit in the 18th century, and his wonderful book entitled, *The Decline and Fall of the Roman Empire*. Is that what I am, a traveller? Reducing in size and significance, the buildings became more practical, as we penetrated this ancient quarter of the city.

Turn right at a stone wall and suddenly, straight in front of us, is this spectacular fountain system. I found out later on, that it was built from stone robbed from the Coliseum, associated with a song about two coins and traditionally a meeting place for anyone who wanted to have a conversation, and not be overheard above the sound of the splashing water. To put it a less romantic way: a meeting place for liars, cheats, conspirators and bigamists. In the fifteenth century, it was possible to hire a lip reader, fluent in two or more languages, though they expected to be paid handsomely. Others were cheaper, but they tended to make the odd mistake, sometimes causing misunderstandings, leading to family feuds, war and the death of countless innocent women and children.

Not the right area for spaghetti houses, our hunger was growing. When in doubt, ask a policeman, and I had just seen one. Whether he was *Carabiniere*, gendarmerie, *Polizia di Stato,* state police, *Guardia di Finanza,* financial police, *Polizia Municipale,* city police, or one of the others, I did not know. I had seen them all on different occasions, they were all heavily armed, wearing tight trousers and mostly in leather boots. When I asked someone the difference between *Polizia di Stato* and Carabiniere, I was informed that *Carabiniere* were slightly more stupid. Can you imagine financial police in England; tax inspectors with machine guns. I walked up to him and asked him politely, in my best broken English, if he knew where we could buy a cheap plate of spaghetti. He swept his hand through the air, as if to dismiss me while keeping his eyes fixed on the building in front of him.

I assumed he hadn't heard me, thought I was a local, or hadn't understood me. To deal with these issues at once, I raised my voice and said, *"scusi,"* which I had already found out meant excuse me. Every time I repeated it, the slashing movement with his right arm became more vigorous, all the time never taking his eyes off the door to this building. Within seconds the door burst open, and two men walked out. Several police appeared from various directions, with guns pointing at the frightened men, who tumbled out of the building, and immediately raised their hands. I had witnessed an attempted robbery of the Banka Nationale Agricole, or Farmer's bank as we would call it over here. The last *"scusi"* trailed out of my mouth, and I decided to ask someone else for directions.

Eventually we found an area of the city that seemed to specialise in cheap bowls of spaghetti, with the waiters touting for business in the street. The price always seemed to be 200 lira, the competitive edge being gained by the volume on offer, or their knowledge of English. Funny they all knew I was English, since family and friends had always told me I looked a bit Italian. I was drawn to an offer by a waiter who said *"You can ave glass of wine fur naught"*. Shot down over Libya, he spent several years as a prisoner of war in Wales, building meaningless dry stone walls. A bit puzzled by his accent, which was not Welsh, I moved on to the spaghetti. Why do they always give you a spoon when they find out you are not Italian?

Full to the gunwales with spaghetti, and, after more than a couple of espressos, we made our way to the central station, to see about the next bit of our journey to Naples. There was a train, no time to buy a ticket, just run for it. No problem with the conductor, we can just explain the situation, and take it from there. Soon the conductor was there, asking for our tickets. I said, "Terribly sorry, don't have a ticket," as I passed him a folded 10 Lira note. (Espresso cost 80 Lira.) He said, "Leave the train at the next station." I said, "It would be marvellous, if you would take my name and address and send me the bill, then I will pay it". He said *"Non."* I said "Can I buy a ticket from you?". "Off." As a last resort, I took out my passport, and read to him the bit: "Her Britannic Majesty's etc., request and demands, (I emphasised this bit) .....pass freely etc.."

The station we were ejected onto, belonged to a town that, if I understood correctly, was famous for industrial quantities of pig fat. The smell of the town made me consider becoming a vegetarian for the first time. The evening was pretty grim and uneventful, apart from an argument in a café, related to the word *subito*. I had been told that *subito* meant something along the lines of *Why should I bother serving you*. I later found out I had been given misinformation, and was eventually able to enjoy a coffee in Italy, without an argument.

We found somewhere to bed down for the night, under some kind of wooden platform, at the end of a warehouse. A good night's sleep but a scary awakening soon after dawn. I found myself looking up the exhaust of several commercial vehicles, reversing towards us at speed. They stopped inches before our heads, as I began to realise we had been sleeping under a loading bay, and these guys were probably on commission delivering urgently needed quantities of pig fat. Glad to be on the next available train out.

Not Henley-on-Thames.

Well, I had never experienced anything like the port of Naples. Nor had I seen such levels of heat, physical activity, sweat, aggression and apparent confusion. Wandering around the back streets, I noticed a surprisingly high level of deprivation and squalor, with many street urchins hanging around. People cooking their fish in the streets, and old ladies in black taking in the last bit of sun, before retiring to their dark and gloomy apartments, until the next morning sun. This is the state it was handed back to the Italians, when the war-weary Americans finally left.

Lucky Luciano put himself forward, from his prison cell, as a volunteer to help clear Italy of the Nazi influence. The Americans accepted, and he was parachuted into Sicily, behind enemy lines. Although his family roots were in the local Mafia group called the Camorra, in Naples, he had associates in Sicily, able to recruit operatives from the local population. If one of his associates' approach to a local was rejected, he would simply say, "Lucky would not be happy with that." That was usually enough.

Lucky, I'm on first names now, was a constant and big headache for Hitler. When he continued his efforts in Naples, he had his whole family around him, and he really helped to rip open, what Churchill called, *the soft underbelly of Europe.* When victory came, he got busy with his own enterprises. First came the black market dealings with the *Big Box,* which was an American style shopping mall built to service the US troops. Next came slavery type prostitution, drugs, money laundering, protection, gambling and waste disposal. Waste disposal involves mixing toxic waste with domestic waste, and setting fire to it, by the roadside, resulting in dangerous pollution. This may have killed more people than all his other crimes put together.

The Camorra was a loosely knit group of clans or families that had divided up the city into their territories. They would go about their business with little interference from the police or politicians, who were often on their payroll. The huge amount of men and material the Americans brought to the area, and often left behind, was the springboard for Lucky to become the Capo, and expand his territory with copious amounts of cutting, shooting, stabbing and slicing.

Continuing my stroll around the poor areas, it was possible to see where one family's territory ended, and another began. One area might have many Bureau de Changes, a good solid way to launder money, whereas the next might be big on nightlife. One area would be clean and well organised, yet a few yards further on, the rubbish clearly hadn't been collected for weeks. An edgy but fascinating place to visit, but I'm glad I lived in Henley-on-Thames.

Arriving at the port of Palermo, fairly late in the day, we walked out of town looking for a place to bed down for the night. Myself and my fellow traveller from back home, had a running competition to try to sleep in the most unusual places, something we had often done in England. I had already managed under a honeysuckle bush, beside the Coliseum in Rome, unforgettable for the effect the aroma had on my sense of well-being. We saw our chance to sleep in the middle of a dual carriage-way. I knew it was safe because it had been covered with sheepskins, presumably as part of the drying process.

As always, I fell asleep and managed to sleep through the collection of the sheepskins after their time in the sun. Only stirring, when confronted by an enormous Scammell Scarab, a British made huge three-wheeled tractor unit. Great name but a fairly useless vehicle. In fact there was probably no danger and we had done it, we had slept on the fast lane of a motorway. Next time you are tanking along the motorway and you see a solitary figure standing on a bridge, it could be me, dreaming of my youth.

Sunday afternoon in Palermo seemed a little dull. Everything shut, no one was around. After several circuits of the central area, I said to Hugh "Do you fancy going to the cinema this evening?" He said "Depends what's on. No point in going if we can't understand a word they are saying." It was *The Italian Job,* which had just been released and was destined to become a classic. We checked on the times, and hung around for the commencement of the evening performance. Sitting on the stone steps, I noticed how they had been worn into a U shape, by the passage of a never ending stream of cinema goers, over countless aeons. Either that, or they were made out of substandard stone, as supplied by a local well known firm.

Before long, people started arriving on foot, and cars began drawing up, until the whole area became busy. I couldn't help but notice all the punters were male. It did cross my mind that *The Italian Job* might be like *The French Job,* but probably not, as it was starring Michael Caine. Time for us to buy our tickets and take our seats. I didn't exactly get what the man in the kiosk was saying, but I did understand he didn't want to sell us tickets. I think it was some kind of grand opening night for local dignitaries.

At that very point, several large limousines pulled up, and the drivers got out to open the car doors. All the men had their jacket buttons undone, indicating they were armed, or *packing*, as I now call it. Only one person was left in the back of the black limo, fat with a fat cigar. A family get-together, or an outing of the local cement firm's senior management? As they breezed past us the ticket seller seemed less interested in arguing with me and sold us our tickets. I followed in their wake and took my seat, a few rows behind. It seemed to be a requirement to smoke in this cinema, so I pulled out my last pack of *Black Africa*.

I spent half my time watching this family. It soon became obvious who the boss was. A slight tilt of his head and an instruction could be whispered into a waiting ear. "Peach ice cream. Clip the ear of that youth who is spitting his orange pips in my direction." That sort of thing. At the end of the film a huge roar of laughter and applause filled the cinema, and we all started to leave. On the way out the usher must have told of our Englishness, and the man himself came up to us, pinched my cheek and gently slapped my face, before ordering me a strawberry ice cream.

We were on a mad dash to cross Europe, on the *Super Rapido Express,* and get to Africa, before my crime in Nice was tied up with illegal entry into France and Interpol was passed the case. I was now hobnobbing with a powerful and ruthless crime boss, who looked like the spitting image of my Grandpa. Years from now I might probably be ashamed of my crime, but for now, I was on the ship heading to Africa.

A Blonde Ukrainian Man.

Still slightly confused by the situation, and not a little excited, the ship approaches the distant shores of Africa. Figures start moving across the deck, as passengers begin gathering themselves, and their baggage, into what they perceive as pole position for a swift disembarkation. Days of inactivity transform into haste and anxiety, as the shoreline begins to define itself. Unidentified cartons of various shapes appear on deck, along with ageing relatives on guard duty. An enormous flock of pink flamingos, apparently pink because of their taste for shrimps, rise up from the bay, as we turn a little starboard and head up an inlet.

As I was saying..... pink flamingos, long inlet, people moving around the docks, and my first sight of Africa, Tunisia in fact, but that didn't mean a lot to me at the time. I was surprised by the number of Arabs walking about the place. Some kind of guest worker situation, like Germany, I thought. No sign of the locals anywhere, which I thought was a bit odd. Just all these Arab guest workers and their wives and their children.... loads of them.

I sat on the quayside, enjoying the sun, and watching the ship being unloaded. I was joined by a tall, well dressed, blond man, in his early twenties. He introduced himself, "I am Carl, first from the Ukraine, but now from *Deutschland.*" He was waiting around to supervise the unloading of his car, which was a white Triumph Spitfire, and a small cargo of what turned out to be a selection of shoe samples, all left foot, and assorted resistors and condensers. He was, however, completely and utterly penniless, flat broke or as he explained it *"Nix fluse"*.

As the day was getting on, we agreed to team up together, and go looking for a cheap hotel. We drove around for a while, until we came across a road block, manned by heavily armed military wearing plimsolls, some of them teenagers. It was hard to figure out what they wanted. My best broken-English didn't work, so I resorted to my broken French. One of the guards got into the car and directed us to a police post. There, they set the angle of the car headlights, and let us proceed. It is funny how these things seem normal at the time, yet bizarre when one looks back. The whole of the road system, as it existed at the time, was like a moving scrap heap, and yet they had become obsessed with the setting of headlights!

We made our way down to *Centre Ville,* and parked in *Place Sidi Bayanne.* One of the locals, OK I now realised they were not guest workers, agreed to look after the car all night for a fee of two left shoes. We took the electronic components and our personal things and went looking for somewhere to spend the night. *Hotel de la Poste* looked like it might be our price range so we decided to give it a go. A beautiful example of a rotting, abandoned empire and about the right price.

We spent several days in Tunis before heading East. Sleeping in a Triumph Spitfire is a skilled and delicate matter, that never has a good outcome, but we did get to know our Ukrainian friend well. There was just about room for two, but not three, so I headed off on my own. I left Hugh and our new found Ukrainian friend and carried on alone.

There is this Arab thing that does not allow them to pass a hitch-hiker, so the wait for a lift was short. We drove across a vast desert of fine sand, along a road that was dead straight and probably Roman, so I dozed. I always find myself dozing on Roman roads. At some point the driver nudged me, and I was confronted by this huge amphitheatre, far better preserved than the one in Rome, probably because the stone hasn't been robbed to build fountains. This formed a roundabout in the middle of the desert. I have since found out this is El Jem. At the time devoid of any houses, but probably destined to become a tourist hot spot.

Next stop Libya. Here are some facts: More than half the size of Kazakhstan, bigger than Mozambique and Paraguay put together, yet with a population of less than 2 million souls, which is the current population of the Kingdom of Eswatini. I was told the main export was scrap metal from the second world war tank battles. Seeing the fields of blown up tanks and trucks I can believe it. It has to be the best possible place for two World Powers to thrash it out, with little damage to the environment.

At the time of my visit, King Idris was on the throne, but I heard from a member of the secret service - jeans and leather jacket were the give-away - he was hoping his general Gaddafi would soon be running the shop, after overthrowing the King. I couldn't see it happening myself. The people were very friendly and hugely hospitable, although most young men seemed to be homosexual. I think it is more of a cultural thing, since sex with women is not allowed before marriage. Rather like pederasty in Ancient Greece, where it was acceptable and common if there was a good age gap, and totally unacceptable if not. In Libya it was quite normal to see soldiers, walking in the park, hand in hand.

The short hop to the capitol, Tripoli, took less than a day. I was dropped by my driver, on the outskirts of the city, around dusk. Resting in a cafe, eating olives and drinking Libyan milk, (basically frothy milk with a dash of coffee - probably the only thing left by the Italians after they raped the country), I was getting to know the locals. Around the corner came a squad of heavily armed US marines. They looked enormous. They came to a halt and a small party broke off, and approached me. One on either side picked me up, and moved me to the centre of the squad, and frog-marched me down the street, to the nearest tourist hotel, telling me to, "Be careful son". Of course I was too young and naïve to notice any threat, and too small to threaten anyone. Even when approached by beggars, often with their hands cut off, I would raise my boot, made of Spanish leather, and flap the broken sole at them. They would either leave me alone, or make a small donation. Worn footwear, or none at all, are a universal sign of poverty.

I didn't take to Tripoli, so I soon moved on towards Benghazi, a distance of over 630 miles, on the R3, as the Romans called their main road across Africa. My first lift of the day was two professors of antiquity, from the University in Tripoli, on a mission to Leptis Magna, to sketch and translate the graffiti on the walls of the public toilets. I knew the name from the local brand of cigarettes, but that was the extent of my knowledge. Take an average Libyan professor of ancient archaeology, and ask him "What happened here?" I promise the results will be magic.

One arrives at Leptis Magna with very little prior warning. Very few buildings, no signage and no tourist infrastructure. Suddenly it's there, it's massive, and it's beautiful. Surrounded on three sides by the type of sand that looks and feels like it has escaped from an egg timer, and bordered by the deep blue of the Mediterranean.

Founded by the Phoenicians it fell under Roman control, after their defeat in the Punic wars. The Roman Republic sent some colonists, together with a small garrison, to protect them and control the city. Merchants soon followed, realising there was a good trade to be done with the surrounding rich farmland. By 49 BC, exactly 2000 years since I was born, annual olive oil production had reached three million and fifty tons. Had one year's production been stockpiled, and consumed in equal proportions over the last 2000 years, it would have provided 1500 tons per year. A lot of oil.

The Roman Emperor Tiberius, who you may remember from your history lessons as the one who trained infants, he called *my little fish,* to swim naked with him in his bath, and nibble on his genitalia, incorporated the Leptis Magna and surrounding farmlands into the Empire. The City grew and soon became one of the leading cities in Roman Africa. Emperor Nero, soon after his marriage to the freedman Pythagoras, in which Nero plays the role of bride, wearing the bridal veil and carrying nuptial torches, commissioned the amphitheatre, just before he sent his Praetorian Guards on a expedition up the Nile to prepare for the invasion of Ethiopia, but that's another story.

One of the professors suggested he stand in the middle of the amphitheatre, as I sit at the top,
while he speaks at normal voice levels. It was possible to hear him with remarkable clarity. From here, there is a fabulous view of the city, and a realisation that we were the only three people in the whole city. Almost no one seems to know about this place or come here, it is as though it has yet to be discovered by the wider world.

As we strolled towards the port area, in the intense heat, it was explained to me that the port could handle up to 300 ships in any one day. Loading: ivory, wild animals and grain, Libya was regarded as the breadbasket of Rome. We continued on to the Arch of the Emperor Septimus Serverus. He was born here, died in York, and, when he became emperor, set about making Leptis Magna as great and as beautiful as Rome. He nearly succeeded in the first objective, and definitely succeeded with the latter.

Turning right we pass an area of unexplained empty space. In a blinding flash I connected a link between our Boxing Day family walk around Virginia Water, where I saw the name *Leptis Magna* on a plaque by some Roman pillars. All that stone had travelled to Fort Belvedere before finally laying in rest in Richmond park, just by the A30. Will anyone ever take them back and refill the empty space in this, once great, city?

The city took a turn for the worst when the 365 tsunami hit. Then it was demolished by the Vandals and rebuilt by the Byzantines. Under the Byzantines, Christianity spread as far south as the land of *Garamantes* in Fezzan. *Garamantes*, you may remember, is a desert kingdom that spanned five million square miles. They built their kingdom by cattle herding, farming dates, and hunting Ethiopian cave-dwellers, but they are remembered in history because of their *qanat* irrigation system. A system to bring fossil water to the surface, and move it along underground aqueducts, thus avoiding evaporation. After six centuries, the fossil water reserve dried up, and the kingdom declined, leaving almost nothing of their culture behind.

As the two professors toddled off to conduct their survey of the toilets, I had my time alone. Time to stroll the streets and sit on the bench, once frequented by retired centurions. I was informed it had a reputation among the Citizens of Rome, as the best place to retire. Warm weather, beautiful surroundings, peace and security, and of course loads of dates. Plenty of gladiatorial duels, or Christian slaughter, to watch on a balmy summer day, or perhaps, a game of *Tic-Tac-Toe* or *Merels* on a wet Monday. Ideal for retirement. Lovely to see the rutted stone streets indicating large traffic flows. We now know the Romans drove on the left. This was confirmed by examining the wheel ruts leading to a quarry. The ruts on the left side were deeper, confirming the heavily laden carriers exited the quarry on the left side.

Land and water mismanagement, and a dryer period of climate, meant the writing was on the wall. Centuries of overgrazing by the Muslim Arabs goats and camels, on their unstoppable march to complete the *Green Crescent* and meet up in Central Europe, completed the desertification. So the desert moved in, and the people moved out, and Leptis Magna remains a stunning example of how our cities may look in the future. By the way, the toilet block was a disappointment. Nothing decipherable or worth sketching. Presumably hit badly by the Vandals.

Another Beautiful Cities, Gone Now.

I said my goodbyes to my friends and stuck my thumb out. In no time at all, a truck driver, carrying supplies for the burgeoning oil industry, picked me up. He was travelling at no more than a fast cycle speed, had a broken windscreen and lots of missing parts. I was not looking forward to the grinding 896 km slog to the regional capital of Benghazi. I took the opportunity to further develop my desert-crossing mind set, which involved long snoozes and much gazing at sand dunes, wondering what the lifestyle of Bedu was really like, and if I should adopt it.

In three hours of enduring the dust, heat and noise, we had made about 60 km, so we parted company at the first available town of Ad Dafiniyah. I found a dirt-cheap place to spend the night, and set off to find a dirt-cheap place to eat. This took the form of a shack, serving unidentifiable round lumps of meat, washed down by strong, sweet, black tea. The proprietor explained it was not everyday fare, but his daughter was married a few days ago, and this was left over. It was camel's hump, sliced sheep's anus, or it could have been goat's vagina, and soup with eye-balls in it. It was this that first made me consider turning vegetarian.

On the road, early the next morning, I picked up a fantastic lift. Lovely car, driven by a lovely educated man with a good knowledge of English. Speed was limited because of the occasional sand dune, half blocking the road. This could be tricky because the edges of the road were still heavily seeded with Second World War mines. Nevertheless, good progress was made to where my kind driver dropped me off, perhaps 200 km short of Benghazi.

I don't remember the name of this town but I do remember how dusty it was. I sat drinking tea and watched a bus pull up. As the door opened, sand poured out to form a pyramid, perhaps a yard high. We had tracked the tail end of a sand storm, and it had got everywhere, including in my eyes. It was late afternoon, and as I began my search for somewhere to stay, I was beginning to realise my sight was going. It became too painful to open my eyes, and if I did, I couldn't see a lot anyway. I now know I was suffering from sand/sun blindness, known as *photo-keratitis*, a kind of sunburn on your eyeballs. It was scary, but after a couple of hours of sitting in a dark room, my sight began to return. By morning I just had sore eyes.

I plodded on, through Benghazi without stopping, on and on. I always have to keep moving, as though I was in a hurry to reach my next destination. But I had no destination, in fact I never really knew where I was, or where I was going. I've always had patience and a strong curiosity, but it's often trumped by this motion thing. The downside is that sometimes,

I miss out on things by not staying around long enough. I put it down to the childhood accident I had on my swing, when I split my head open and needed three stitches. It must have adjusted my brain in just the area that controls motion, probably sense of direction and spelling as well. Soon after Benghazi we leave the beautiful Bay of Cyrene and head inland over some mountains, stopping for the night at Shahat.

After a breakfast of Libyan milk, yoghurt with honey and bread, with camel-milk cheese, I head for the road. The first thing I see is a wonderful Roman portico, carved into the living rock. I had stumbled upon the city of Cyrene. I mean I'm not saying I was the first to see it since the abandoned ruins were passed over by the Arab Conquest around 643 AD, but I had no idea it was here, but here it was.

This portico led to a dwelling of elegant proportions and considerable size. There was no gate or other security, so I wandered around the various rooms. I left with the impression it had been the home of a wealthy trader of some sort. Possibly a grower or dealer in *silphium*. *Silphium* was the mainstay of trade in Cyrene, since as far back as its foundation as one of the five cities called *Pentapolis* by the Greek king of the island of Thera.

Silphium was a sticky dark resin that was extracted from the plant, and used as seasoning, perfume, aphrodisiac, abortifacient and had unspecified recreational uses. There is some indication it was a hallucinogen. One of the many strange things about *silphium* is that it would only grow in an area within 100 miles of Cyrene. If grown from seed, the resulting plant would not have seeds. It may have been a type of fennel. The enormous demand from the Roman Empire resulted in overharvesting, and the particular quality required for recreational use could no longer be grown, so the plant eventually became extinct. The last block of Cyrene *silphium* resin, stamped with its own glyph, and the last known stalk was given to Emperor Nero as a souvenir.

Cyrene is also famous for being the city where the first Roman-Jewish war kicked off. The Jews had been used to receiving equal treatment, from their *Ptolemaic* rulers, for hundreds of years, until Rome took over and oppressed them. As part of their fight back, the *Sicarii* came to prominence. They were an organised group of assassins that carried a small dagger under their cloaks (think cloak and dagger). Their method was simple~ mix in a large crowd, pull out your dagger and kill a Roman, before disappearing back into the crowd.

I bought some olives and bread, and wandered down to the City Centre to enjoy my lunch, sitting on a stone bench, in the Temple of Apollo. A short stroll around the eight square kilometre *Necropolis* and I'm back on the road waiting for a lift. Really waiting for the next vehicle, because almost everyone will stop for me. It was the next vehicle, but it took more than an hour to arrive. Asked if I wanted to go to Tobruk I said yes please. Just 250 km away, I should make it before dusk.

Egyptian border.

The last few miles was a taste of things to come. Hundreds of blown-up, burnt out and bombed tanks and other military vehicles, some reasonably intact, others just a skeleton. Many recycled as sheds, food stores, a shop and many strange looking carts with oversized wheels. Not much left of Tobruk really, partly due to the efforts of the Australian *Rats of Tobruk*. It was originally built by the ancient Greeks as a defensive position for Cyrene, before serving the same purpose for many other invading armies. The ancient Greeks name for Tobruk roughly translates as, *Across the sea from Crete,* like we might refer to Australia as *down under,* but reversed.

Not the most interesting place to spend the night. Can't imagine why King Idris would want to build his palace here. I hope they rebuild the town some day. It gets exciting now though, I have just heard Egypt is less than 150 km from here. My driver, whom I understood to be a Libyan customs official, has warned me that the border may be difficult, since the breakdown of the United Arab Republic, which had united Egypt, Libya and other states in 1958. He was right, there was no traffic.

After a couple of hours waiting, I decided to take up his offer of a glass of mint tea and a floor to sleep on, for which I was grateful. During the warm night I was aware of a crunching noise every time I turned over, but I was far too tired to investigate further. In the morning it became clear what the crunching noise was about. I had been rolling on numerous large black beetles known as *The Egyptian beetle,* or *scarabaeus*. Although fearsome looking and incredibly strong (if I had their strength I would be able to lift a Scammell Scarab with one hand) they do not eat human flesh, only dung.

The very name, Egypt, sounds so magical I expected something to change at the border, but it was a *ruler drawn* border on a map in the middle of the desert, and not much changed. The surly border guards gave me a hard time about the lack of some documents. I thought it was a yellow fever certificate that was needed, so I retired for a while, and printed one, with my John Bull Printing outfit, and some blank yellow fever cards I had picked up at my doctors surgery in Henley. In the end it didn't work, so I tried my AA International

Driving Licence. That worked a treat, probably because it had a photo and was translated into many languages, including Arabic, although I doubt he could read. I had 500 km more desert to look forward to, before I reached Alexandria, with very little to see on the way. Egypt has around half the population of Britain, and 90% of those live on the Nile, so seeing *anyone* was surprising.

Alexandria was a bustling place and I was pleased to be here. I was directed to the Hotel de Paris at the eastern end of the Corniche, which is the waterfront. I always liked the name Corniche, probably because it sounded like Cornish. The hotel was owned by a very old French lady who smoked Gauloise and wore black. I never scratched the surface but I bet she had a hell of a story to tell.

I travelled back to the city centre on a double decker tram, which looked like one of those buses they used on the Western Front during WW1, with the spiral stairs. The system was built towards the end of the nineteenth century and electrified at the beginning of the twentieth century. The ageing cars were covered in equally ageing advertisements for Lipton's Tea and Woodbine cigarettes, among other products. In spite of the minimal cost of a ticket, many people clung to the outside for free. Children, with smaller fingers, could jump on the rear and stick their finger in the grill, sometimes at the cost of little fingers.

I was getting used to seeing almost all young men and boys wearing pyjamas in the street. Proper striped pyjamas, made of thick cotton with a tie cord around the waist, just like we used to wear in the fifties. Probably some British manufacturer produced a batch, not up to the specifications of the retailer, and they were jobbed out to a buyer in Egypt, happy to buy anything if the price was right. A similar thing happened in Bolivia. A trader found a large batch of bowler hats (manufactured in Manchester and destined for British engineers in Bolivia) were too small. He jobbed them out to market traders, who in turn sold them to local *Aymara* women. The trend became entrenched in their society, and they are now worn as part of the national dress, on the side of the head for single or widowed women and on the top for married women.

No Remorse.

After a few days I set out on the 230km journey to Cairo, leaving the Roman road, the R3, after many weeks. The Romans said it was the second best road in the Empire, and I could only agree. The road to Cairo went through the heart of the verdant Nile Delta, with its endless productive farms stretching as far as the eye could see. It was interesting watching the local farmers, known as *Fellah,* go about their work, unchanged for thousands of years. The *Fellah* are proud of their direct link with the *ancients*. One day they may be able to prove it with some kind of blood matching, with the mummies or, some yet to be invented, scientific advancement.

Still with many miles to go, the Great Giza Pyramids (A Greek word meaning oat cake) appear on the horizon. My first impression was how perfectly formed they were, with no sign of any blemishes, due to the considerable distance. It is a testament to their size that they grow so slowly, as we approach at a reasonable speed. My lift is taking me to the centre of Cairo, so we pass them by for now, and head for an area famous for cheap hotels.

Today is 3 June 1967, and it is hot. I'm up at the crack of dawn and off to find, what I have been led to believe, is the oldest cafe in Cairo. Of course the sun is shining, but it is not yet hot. The early mornings start off quite chilly, and as the temperature rapidly rises, there is a period, lasting perhaps no more than half an hour, when the temperature is just perfect. I did find the cafe and had a lovely breakfast. The cafe, called El-Fishawy, is famous because it had no doors, so had never shut since it first opened in 1797. According to legend it was frequented by Napoleon Bonaparte during the French occupation of Egypt. Apparently he loved eating and drinking on tables in the street, and adopted the idea for Paris.

After breakfast, I negotiated a shared taxi and headed for Giza. I was dropped-off close to the pyramids and decided to walk around Khufu's great pyramid. By now it was approaching midday, which is when the British go out to look at stuff. I took on the challenge of walking round the base. I know it doesn't sound like much of a challenge, but it was hot and big, and I hadn't yet learnt to take water with me. But I made it and I will never forget the experience. I climbed some way up. The blocks are enormous, perhaps up to ten feet high so it's not easy.

Words fail me, so I will quote others: "Where Time hath dropped his scythe, and furled his wings" Nicholas Mitchell. "Forty centuries looking down at me" Napoleon Bonaparte. "Gimme 30,000 disciplined workmen, and 30 years and I'll build a bigger one." American engineer working on the Assam Dam. Size is beyond belief. I was told Napoleon's *Servants* calculated there would be enough stone in the Great Pyramid to build a two metre wall around France. Shut the kitchen door!

Back in my gloomy hotel room, I found time to reflect. I should be full of remorse for my crime on the boat from

Gibraltar, but I didn't even think about it. Shame and remorse were set aside for later. I should be lonely, since I had not spoken to an English person for weeks, but it never crossed my mind. I had taken some risks, and been to some dangerous places, but I had no fear. Not really brave, just naïve. I simply wasn't aware of the danger, which is perhaps why it never touched me. I was a boy, discovering the world by myself and in my own way. Since I had left school at the age of fifteen, barely able to read or write, this was like my time at university. I was growing up, and learning how to make my way in life. Or was I just a youth going astray?

The next morning I woke up and I wanted to go home. Just an overwhelming feeling of homesickness. So I packed, which usually takes about 3 minutes, and went to check-out. The owner told me he could offer a three-day trip, up the Nile to Luxor at the much reduced price of twenty five Egyptian pounds, about five pounds Sterling. Actually more like two pounds when taking into account the black market rate. He said it would be a wonderful experience to visit Karnak and the Valley of the Kings, and that if I didn't take up his offer I would regret it for the rest of my life. I politely declined his offer, thinking I just couldn't be bothered.

Escape.

It didn't take long for someone to stop and take me all the way to Alexandria, buying me lunch on the way. Once in Alexandria, I walked down the Corniche to the place where the shipping companies had their offices, with a view to booking a ticket to Piraeus, which is the port town of Athens. Unfortunately it was closed, so I took my passport-pouch off my belt, and retrieved my notebook so I could make notes of the times and prices of the passage. Just then, a military convoy came around the corner. I was struck by the tatty uniforms and lack of serviceable boots, some were even wearing thongs. The vehicles were in a similar state, with bald tyres and torn canvas on the roof.

By the time they had passed, I had drifted from the shipping line office, inadvertently leaving behind my passport-pouch containing my passport, money and John Bull printing outfit. Within five minutes, a young man had worked his way through the crowd and found me, and returned it to me, with no suggestion of any buckshee. I had been in these desert lands long enough to develop a huge respect for Arab honesty, their warmth and boundless hospitality.

I returned to the shipping office to buy a one-way deck-class ticket to Athens. While I was in the office, I met a ship's captain, and we started having a conversation. Before he left he said he was having a party this evening and asked if I would like to attend. I accepted the invitation, and we made arrangements for him to collect me from my hotel. The party was in a luxury apartment, right on the Corniche, and was attended by several high-ranking naval personnel, including captains, and at least one admiral. We all proceeded to get blind drunk on whiskey. One of the captains leaned across to me, and said, "Tomorrow we bombard the coast of Israel". It was 5 June and the start of the 6 day war. It did cross my mind that I should pass this information on to someone, perhaps MI5, or the Israel Secret Service known as MOSSAD. I decided they probably knew and it would have given me a moral dilemma anyway.

The next day I walked to the port area. It was chaos. A mass of people clambering to get through customs and onto the next boat out. Just when it would have been helpful to glide through customs, they insisted on seeing my bank receipts, proving that I had changed money officially and not on the black market. My stupidity had come back to bite me. Thank goodness for the secret place in my passport-pouch, where I could hide the cash. Hopefully I will be able to change it into something more useful in Greece. It only remained for me to convince them that I had lived in Egypt on about 1/6d a day.

After passing through customs it all became even more intense, with people pressing against the barrier ,waving their tickets and passports hoping to be let onboard. I followed suit and a Greek officer, from the ship I was hoping to catch, saw me and gestured for me to pass him my passport. He seemed completely amazed and reached for his ID card. Unbelievably he had the same surname as me. My problems were over and I was on board. I know, I wouldn't have believed it either.

There were perhaps forty other passengers travelling deck-class. A motley collection of drifters and travellers, a couple of which were carrying guitars. I was still only just eighteen, so they were all slightly older than me. It was a new and wonderful experience, sitting under the canvas awning that covered most of the deck, listening to the music and watching the striped dolphins tracking the ship. Wonderful to be speaking English to English speakers again.

Coup d'etat, Not Ice Cream.

After three days, and 698 nautical miles, we steamed into Piraeus. Almost on arrival, I started to hear about the Arab-Israeli so-called *Six Day War*. I thought of those lovely naval people, all the kind people I had met in the desert that had looked after me, that young man that had displayed outstanding honesty and integrity, and those soldiers in thongs driving their lorries with bald tyres. Even I could reason that their armed forces were not up to much, and that they would surely lose this war soon enough. It made me sad.

The first thing that struck me about Greece was how clean it was. After weeks in the desert lands it was quite a contrast. The people seemed less than friendly though. I was no longer the centre of attention, and people were not falling over each other to help me. I decided to move quickly through Greece, but I was very short of money. I had heard, from one of the Europeans travelling deck class with me, that it was possible to sell my blood in Greece. I thought I would head to Alexandra General Hospital, and give it a go. When I arrived there they took a sample to test my blood group, since that would apparently have a large effect on the price they would offer.

My blood group came back as O rhesus-negative, also known as the universal blood. The most precious blood on earth, due to the fact that anyone can receive it. It is also known to be the first blood of mankind, with the origins going back to the dawn of human history. According to Japanese legend, people with the gift of this blood group have an exceptionally curious mind, but a bad sense of direction. Really! Of course I was able to negotiate a much higher price, with a lady desperate to save her husband's life.

I gave as much as the nurse would allow, and felt fine afterwards. The Indian man, laying on the bed next to me, gave the same quantity. Unfortunately his blood pressure dipped to a dangerous low point, so much so that he was rushed into the next ward and given an immediate blood transfusion. I am guessing he came out of the transaction quite a few Drachma down. As I left the hospital, there was a small group of desperate relatives begging me to give more blood. Word must have gotten out that I was a universal donor.

I was on a mission to go home, so I started hitching straight away. I stood for hours, with loads of cars passing, until eventually someone picked me up, and dropped me in the regional capital of Larissa. Instantly forgettable but suitable for a night's stay. During the journey, it became clear Greece was not a happy place. The population seemed to be hiding. On arriving at every town or village, there was a white wooden sign across the road, with just the date, 21 April 1967, and an identical one on leaving. Meaningless to me of course.

Another short lift left me stranded on a hill in the middle of nowhere. I waited and I waited. No one was stopping, and it was quite noticeable how they avoided eye contact, one of the key skills in hitch-hiking. After several fruitless hours, a huge, dirty oil tanker came thundering up the hill, at walking pace. In my desperation for a lift I slung my kit bag on my back and jumped onto the steel ladder on the back of the truck, climbing up to the top where I was able to cling onto the filling valve.

There was so much gesticulation from pedestrians and flashing of light from other vehicles, that the driver decided to stop and see what was going on. He was a kind old man who took pity on this teenager and allowed me to enter the cab. It was such an uncomfortable ride, made less so by constantly swigging on a bottle of some kind of home made sweet spirits.

We parted company on the outskirts of Thessalonica. Although it was the second city of Byzantium, there didn't seem to be much of its past charm left. The buildings seem to date post-war, and looked like they were thrown up in a desperate bid to house the many homeless people returning from some war. As I was on a mission to get home, I decided to blow a considerable sum on a ticket for the overnight bus to Sofia. I located the bus stop and was told the bus would arrive around 10:00 pm, and that I should be very careful as there were bad people doing bad things.

I was pleasantly surprised when the bus arrived more than an hour early, but it was packed. I must have had the last seat, located on top of a wheel arch, with little leg room. I was unpleasantly surprised when the bus stopped at the Turkish customs. I had got on the right bus, just going in the wrong direction. Damn those Europeans for driving on the wrong side of the road. I stayed on the same bus and it eventually dropped me at the same place, but on the opposite and *correct* side of the road, before returning to the bus depot.

It must have been a few hours before dawn, but it was warm, so I went looking for a place to sleep. On the modern shopping street, there was a TV shop. Outside the shop, by the curbside, was a large wooden packing case, filled with that manufactured straw-like material they used for protecting fragile goods. Perfect for a short night's sleep.

Just around dawn, I was woken by a huge mechanical thundering noise, with intermittent screeching sounds, like a badly maintained tractor, shortly followed by a continuous thudding noise, like golf balls falling on my crate. I looked through a crack in my crate to observe a column of tanks, hurtling through the high street at speed, throwing up lumps of tarmacadam as they passed. Staying put seemed the safest option.

It soon passed, and shortly afterwards the town began to wake up, with children going to school and people going to work. I started to get ready to leave the safety of my crate, when a schoolboy noticed some movement and gingerly peered into the crate. When I sat up, completely covered in this artificial straw, I must have been a sight. The poor boy took one look and legged it down the road screaming.

My breakfast-cafe owner had a reasonable command of English, so I managed to form a sketchy picture of what was going on. A right wing junta, comprising two colonels and one brigadier, decided to have a right-wing *coup d'etat,* just weeks before the planned election, to *save* the country from a communist take-over. One of the colonels was in command of the Armour Training Centre which explains the widespread use of tanks. They immediately changed the law to allow them to arrest anyone they liked, without charge. There were widespread arrests, torture and executions. What I had seen was a movement of tanks to crush local dissent.

The Junta immediately banned certain things, including men with long hair, mini-skirts, the Beatles, Mark Twain, labour-strikes, peace-symbols, Socrates and the letter Z. Actually it was the American spelling Zee, rather than the English spelling Zed, that was banned, as it apparently translates to *He will rise again,* and probably referred to Georgeios Papaioannou, likely next president but now under house arrest. There were stories of English being picked up and having their heads shaved, followed by a good beating. I considered my options with great care and clarity and decided to get the **** out of here.

Hitch-hiking seemed out of the question so I caught another bus, taking great care to stand on the right side of the road. Six hours to Sofia, change bus and a further gruelling 5 hours on cobblestone roads to Nis (pronounced Nish, and named after the river Nisave which was a name given by a Celtic tribe in 3rd. Century BC) in Serbia. From here it seemed it would be safe to hitch-hike again.

I found a roadside cafe and stopped for a tea. It was the normal Yugoslavian system for cafes, where you had to order and pay at the till for what you wanted, before it was delivered to your table. That works well only if you can speak the language. The cafe would of course be owned by *society,* rather than the state, in their strange, unusual and ultimately rather unsuccessful kind of communism. The cake delivered to my table was in fact a meat pie, and the tea was made from melon seeds, I think.

As I left the cafe, I was detained by a policeman. He checked my passport, went through my belongings with a fine toothcomb, phoned his superiors before letting me go, with a warning to cut my hair. People were becoming more and more afraid of other people with long hair, for no apparent reason.

Turned on.

After several hours of non-stopping cars, a Citroen Deux Chevaux appeared on the horizon. The Deux Chevaux is a wonderful piece of design. It is designed to be cheap, yet robust, and work well on cobblestones, due to the unique type of suspension. Its lack of a water-filled radiator makes it ideal for desert work. Windows are a simple swinging flap, there is a dip-stick rather than a petrol gauge, the speedo works directly from the front wheels and the windscreen-wipers work from the speedo. When travelling along bumpy and rutted roads, it simply sways from side to side like a ship of the desert. The top speed was around 40mph but it was much, much slower uphill. Almost any sort of incline meant changing to first gear and staying in it until one has crested the hill.

There was a slight incline, so this particular car took what seemed like an age to arrive, but it did stop. "Would you like a lift?" "Yes please." There was no conversation about where I was going, or where they were going. I sat in the back with an American called Brad. He was one of the army of 171,000 *Vietnam conscientious objectors*, so was forced into becoming a *drifter* rather than face jail in his own country. The driver was a Frenchman, with shoulder length hair, called Theo, and the passenger an Italian named Francesco.

Francesco was in a hurry to get back to his home in Milan, as he had received word that his father was critically ill. Like most travellers with long hair, affectionately called *Freaks* or *Heads*, they were on their way to India, when he collected the letter from the *poste restante* in Istanbul. The *poste restante* system meant anyone could write a letter, and it would go to the specific post office, in just about any city in the world, where it would wait for the recipient to collect it on payment of a fee. It only worked if you had a plan of where you would be, and most travellers didn't. Mostly, no one knew where you were, and you knew nothing of what was happening back home.

I was a few years younger than these guys, but I was really infatuated with them, and their lifestyle. This was my first encounter with the drug hashish, which we all called *shit*. They were smoking *joints*, also known as *spliffs,* at regular intervals. Brad explained the effect of the drug to me. He told me no one had ever died from the consumption of cannabis, even if taken in excess. I had been smoking cigarettes since I was a 15 year old, on an exchange visit with a French family. They all smoked, from 11 year old Adele upwards. I managed to resist for the whole of my stay, only to succumb on the train journey home, when I smoked a pack I had bought as a present for my Aunt Alice.

I asked Brad if hashish was addictive. He assured me not. Since I was pretty stoned anyway, from the smoky atmosphere, I decided to give it a go. I loved it. We laughed so much I wondered if the car was driven by petrol or laughter. Apparently, they had bought a lump in Istanbul. They had shaped it to fit exactly into a *La Vache Qui Rit* cheese box, to sell in Italy and cover the cost of the return trip to Milan. They fully intended to carry on to India once Francesco's Dad was dead, or out of trouble. I wondered again why I had chosen to go to Africa, when everyone else seemed to be heading to India. Just to avoid complying with what had become a trend, I suppose. To be different, even from people that were already different. Still I hope to get to India someday soon.

Nis to Milan is 1280 km.. It turned out to be one of the most agreeable and amusing journeys of my *Grand Tour* of the Roman Empire. It was summer, so we just slept outside, and mostly ate picnics. On one occasion, we had a small campfire, which we were sitting around, rolling a joint, which Francesco then lit with a 1000 Lira note. It should have been worth about ten shillings, but the government had recalled the notes in another desperate attempt to control inflation, so it was now worth nothing. It was some kind of a sign of disrespect aimed at the Italian Government and *straight* society in general. Looked kind of cool though.

When we arrived at the Italian border, Francesco and Theo were joking that the border guards would have no idea that the cigarette they were smoking was in fact a joint. They were right, and we passed straight through, with not even a cursory glance inside. We travelled as far as Mestre, a lovely town in its own right, but completely overshadowed by Venice, and decided to stay here for a while. We got stoned, had a wonderful and cheap meal organised by Francesco. We then relocated to a beautiful square, where we sat watching the fountains changing colour, and laughing every time it changed to blue, as you do.

The 260 km road to Milan was straightforward and easy, on the recently upgraded surfaces. It should have taken around three hours, but it took all day, due to frequent espresso stops. I had never had espresso before. In the early 1960s, I used to hang out in the Italian coffee bar in Addlestone, during their first wave of popularity, before they disappeared from our High Streets for more than twenty years, but I always had frothy coffee. Stopping to discuss political issues, and important ways in which we were going to change the world, was another form of procrastination. It is now widely accepted that Italians and French are unable to talk without the use of both hands, so espressos were often spilt on clean white table cloths. Francesco later told us that his Dad was having an important operation today, so he would not be able to see him until the morning, which is why we were not in a hurry.

We finally arrived in Milan late in the evening. We drove straight to the house of a lovely English couple, Jay and Rachael. They were probably twice my age, or maybe as old as forty. I had gathered they were in the music business, promoting tours for English bands throughout Italy, but especially in Milan. Jay showed me into this bedroom, with a view to meeting the band. All four of them and the girlfriend of the lead singer were dressed in striped pyjamas, fast asleep in this huge bed.

When I woke in the morning, Francesco and Theo had already left for the hospital, and Brad had set off for some more *drifting*. Jay suggested I go for a walk and get to see a bit of the city. What a beautiful place it is. Hard to imagine such cruelty and ugliness was committed here, less than thirty years ago. I had a lovely few hours wandering, drinking espresso and trying to pick up a bit of the lingo, not without some difficulties though. When asked by the barman if my espresso was *caldo,* I naturally replied no. He changed it twice before refusing to change it a third time. How could *caldo* possibly mean hot? When asked if I would like a *bere* I would respond with "No thank you, a wine please". If *bere* meant drink, what was their word for beer? Strange people.

Back at Jay and Rachael's house, Jay asked if I would like to visit The Jamaica Inn this evening. It was where his band had played last week. Opened in 1911, it was one of the first bars that had an espresso machine and a telephone. It quickly became a haunt for artists and VIPs, including Benito Mussolini himself. The name was changed to Jamaica Inn, after the successful showing of the 1939 English film, *Jamaica Inn,* starring Charles Laughton. Artists would visit to discuss politics, and debate the sex of angles. It was run by the strange eccentric lady, known as Mamma Lina, who refused to accept paintings as payment, so as not to exploit the artist when they were down on their uppers. Apparently the list of wine debtors reads like a who's who of post-war art, film making, photography, literature and intellect.

There was jazz playing that night. It was only the second time I had seen live jazz, the first being at The Bell in Bath in 1965, when it was the place in the South West for jazz music. It was a great evening, with copious amounts of food, wine and pot consumed openly by the clientèle. No change since the 1930s then..

The next morning Francesco and Theo returned. We all went to see Francesco's friend, probably to sell him some dope, but I knew nothing of these things at the time. His friend was apparently heir to *old money* and lived in a slightly fading palace in a beautiful, if slightly overgrown, garden. He also had hair down his back, which was not common in Italy at this time. He had a pet monkey, which I thought was a bit cruel. I suspected he owned it to help create an image of eccentricity, which as we all know, one has to be born with and cannot create. It was dead unhygienic too.

I forgot to say, today is 18th June 1967, and my eighteenth birthday. I am now old enough to drink, but I would have to wait a further three years to vote. The Beatles's *Sergeant Pepper's Lonely Hearts Club Band,* and Pink Floyd's *Piper at The Gates of Dawn,* were released this year; Canada is 100 years old; Keith Richards of The Rolling Stones, is jailed for possession of illegal drugs, and it is no longer a criminal offence for consensual adult (over 21) to be gay.

Going Home.

Theo's Dad was out of the woods, so they would be heading off to India in a week. I was leaving this morning, so I said my farewells and hit the road. After a bus ride out of the city, I did what I did so well and stuck my thumb out. The first car offered me a lift to Stuttgart. It sounded roughly in the right direction so I took it. Actually it was 500km away, and at least 400 km of that was in the right direction.

I had a night in a hostel for guest workers which was basic but friendly. Then back on the road first thing in the morning, in time to catch my first lift from a delivery driver. Where he dropped me was not great. A minor road some way the other side of Stuttgart with very little signs of life. I had no map and really no idea where I was. I waited for a long time with very little traffic. After about two hours, I became a little desperate, so I did what we call a double-hitch. This means I would wait on one side of the road, but if a car came from the other direction, I would cross the road and try to get a lift with that car. Since I didn't know where I was it didn't matter much where the lift took me.

I was lucky, a car pulled up driven by a man, with two youths in the back. He asked a few probing questions and received answers like, "No I didn't think anything is missing," and "No I am not searching for anything." We had always been a very irreligious family, although I did go to Sunday School and loved it. My mother would often say she was envious of people who could believe in life after death. Who wouldn't? Much as I tried, I could not destroy the wall of logic in my brain. I have always loved being in churches though, especially village ones. I had also thought the Christian way of life was good, and similar in many ways to the hippie ideal. Without the pot of course, but often wearing similar clothes and using God speak rather than hippie speak.

In hippie speak one might say, "It would be far-out if we could get some bread together from the other heads and score some Afghan Gold Seal, from a cool scene of freaks. Hope the fuzz isn't there, which would be heavy, especially if you got busted. I'll pick up some skins on the way back to the pad, and we can have a spliff and get off our heads, before I get my shit together and split, which will be a bummer because I don't want to go, but I'm sure it will be groovy when I get there.

After a toke I'll feel mellow and pick up on your vibes, if it doesn't blow my mind. Actually I'm really spaced-out already, but I'm going to keep on truckin. Why not? It's 1967, The Summer of Love, can you dig it?"

In church speak, "It would be uplifting to pass the collection box around the congregation and collect some alms to buy some holy wine from a marvellous purveyor of alcoholic drink. I hope the treasurer doesn't see the wine, which would be uncomfortable. I'll collect some glasses on the way back to the gathering of the faithful, and we can drink the holy wine, and feel enlightened. I will then collect my things and depart, which is sad because I don't want to go, but I'm sure it will be uplifting when I get there. After a glass I'll feel tipsy and pick up on the love, if it doesn't exalt me. Actually I'm already exalted, Why not? It's 1967, The Summer of Love, can you dig it Vicar?".

The driver soon understood I was a lost cause, after which it was fine. He asked if I would like to stay for the night in their monastery or did he mean school? Or it could have been a school in a monastery. I was now almost broke, apart from the money set aside for the Calais to Dover ferry, so I agreed. It was way out in the sticks but well worth the journey, as it turned out. It was a wonderful old building, with perhaps around 100 boys and young men in residence. We all sat in the refectory on carved oak chairs around huge oak tables and ate good, wholesome food and loads of it.

I had a wonderful, peaceful night's sleep in the guest bedroom. It had that familiar smell one finds in boy's prep schools with an added layer of fresh bread and oak. I was woken early by bells ringing and footfall. Moving down the ancient oak staircase to breakfast, in the same hall we ate in last night, around the same oak table, I was just in time for grace. Surprisingly my irreligious parents had always insisted we say grace before eating, so I was good at that. It was a lovely breakfast, with everything one would expect at a five-star hotel, with the addition of a huge selection of bread. There was rye-wheat, whole grain, wheat-rye, and best of all, King Ludwig bread, which is made from spelt, wheat flour, rye, and malt. I was allowed to pack as much bread as would fit into my duffel-bag. Just as well as there would be precious little else for the duration of my homeward bound trip.

The kind man who gave me a lift last night, (I found out he was the housemaster,) offered to drop me near the *Autobahn*. I learnt that *Autobahn* is the German motorway system that famously has no speed limit. In fact the world land speed record on a public road was broken in 1938, when 432 kph was reached along a stretch where the bridges were designed not to have any central pillars, in case of an accident. My first lift was in a Mercedes and I set my own speed record at 180 kpm. Needless to say there have been some spectacular crashes, one involving more than 100 vehicles that caught fire and ended up as a huge block of metal welded together.

I noticed we passed many signs to the city of *Ausfahrt* which I assumed must be a huge city. I was dropped at the French border where I found a spot for a King Ludwig lunch before walking across the frontier into France. Only 630 km to Calais, so I pressed on, soon getting a lift from a Dutch water engineer, who had been giving a lecture at the *Commission for*

Navigation on the Rhine on, unsurprisingly, flood defences. A very pleasant man who had but one fault, he was a Dutch man going home, and therefore not going in quite the right direction.

I was dropped off in Maastricht, near the industrial area. I wandered around looking for a suitable place to sleep and eventually found an ideal spot, at the back of a warehouse under a wooden platform. Sleeping rough was very much a part of the journey and it didn't bother me in the least bit, especially not in the summer. I was woken at sunrise by this enormous coordinated roaring sound. I had slept under another loading bay and a formation of large lorries were reversing up to it. Sometimes the worst bit of sleeping rough is the embarrassment of waking up somewhere that looks completely different to how it looked when you bedded down. The drivers made the assumption that I was a poor destitute vagrant. In fact I was a middle-class destitute vagrant, so they felt sorry for me and gave me a large cup of Dutch coffee. The other advantage of sleeping under a loading bay of a logistics company is that I was able to go to the traffic manager's office, and find a lift that was as close as possible to Calais or Ostend.

It was dark when I arrived in Ostend because of all the delivery drops on the way, so I was looking for a suitable place to have supper, only rye-wheat left, and bed down for the night. After walking around for a while I found a nice-looking spot in the form of a wooden landing stage at the quayside. I lay down on this balmy evening, but in the middle of the night a storm brewed up. It was incredible and probably dangerous. High winds, lashing rain and substantial waves battered the landing stage, with me clinging to it, which is what I had to do.

Still dripping wet and now hungry, I stood at the roadside with my thumb sticking out. God was I miserable. I had probably reached a new low point. Then the sun came out and I started to dry off. In no time I had a lift to Dunkirk, a place that had seen far more misery than even I could summon up. Only 43 km to Calais, but I could not get a lift. After trying for at least two hours I decided to go by tram. I thought I might get away with it like I had done as a child in England, by giving my name and address and asking them to send the bill there. Even if it didn't work, the worst that could happen was me being thrown off, closer to Calais. Or a cup of coffee and a croissant in the local gendarmerie. In fact it worked and I got to Calais and down to the ferry terminal.

I waited, bought my ticket and boarded. I was hungry, damp and my packet of cigarettes, I was smoking Camel now because I thought of myself as a junior explorer, were also damp. The only money I had left was a commemorative 1965 Winston Churchill Crown given to me by my Aunt Alice as a keepsake. I changed it at face value, possibly another crime, and spent the money on fags.

We steamed into Dover on a bright and clear sunny day. I made my way through the port area, heading to the main road. As I was walking along, a VW bus pulled up. *"A VW bus, now that's a good idea.* The driver wound down his window and said, "Hey man," he felt he could use those words because I had long hair and a full-set beard. "Hey man, any idea which turning we should take to board the ferry?" I said, "Where are you going?" He replied, "Calais, then on to India," I replied, "Past the big building on the right, then turn left I think."

West End Club.

After a few days of washing, eating, washing clothes and sleeping, I was ready to go out and face the world. I would go down the pub and see who was about. They would buy me drinks and ask me about the places I had seen, the adventures I had enjoyed, and the hardship I had endured. They would be interested to know about the countries I had been to and the people I had met. What I got was: "Hello Paul, haven't seen you for a while. Coming to Jake's party tomorrow?" Nobody was the least bit interested.

I needed some money to go on another trip, so I needed a job. I found one pretty quickly, drilling for water. It involved working away from home, living in a wooden garden-shed type hut, with two or three other workers. The job was about as mindless as the others. Doing things like taking hourly night time readings during a pump test, or bolting on new sections of pipe. All stuff that a well trained Orangutan could carry out at half the cost. My young work mates were fine but the old ones were odd, to say the least.

I stuck it out for a few weeks and enjoyed the high pay. Of course I was spending nothing much during the week, so I found I could save. In fact I saved enough to pass my driving test and buy my own old car. Passing my driving test in Henley-on-Thames was easy. Just before I took it, a driving instructor came to me and said, "Just a tip lad. If he asks you what's the most important thing concerning safety say, *Looking in my mirror before signalling and changing lanes.* He has a thing about that this week." He did ask me that question and I gave the correct answer. He smiled, apparently most unusual, and gave me a pass on my first test, also unusual.

I could now drive to my place of work and have some kind of freedom during the week. I still managed to save plenty of money, so I was wondering where I would travel next. I had this idea of a fairly short trip in the summer. One I could do within the tight exchange control, that limited the amount of money that could be taken out of the country to £65. For no apparent reason I set my mind on Sweden. I knew nothing much about the place, which is the best way to be when you visit a country for the first time. Yes. I would go first to Denmark then over to Sweden.

I handed in my notice and worked my last week. At the weekend I decided to drive to my grandparents for a quick visit, before I left on my next trip. My old car was probably produced in the 1950s or maybe even earlier. The maker's logo had dropped off the front so I am not sure what make it is. I know it was built before 1955, because it had old style trafficators that were used before flashing light indicators were invented. Unfortunately, someone joining the roundabout did not notice these lit arms that proudly poked out the side of my car, indicating my next move and drove into the side of me, wrecking both vehicles. He gave me his card on which was printed *Special sales manager for Molly Mops*, and I gave him my address. I drove my car to the nearest tip and sold it for £5 and left the country.

I left England in early summer of 1967, and set about hitching north to Hull. My plan extended no further than taking *The Peninsular and Oriental Steam Navigation Company* ferry from Hull to Rotterdam, and hitching the 500 odd miles to Copenhagen. It proved to be a doddle, with the added bonus of a ferry ride from Puttgarden in Germany, across the Fermer Baelt to Denmark. This service offered a fixed price *Smorgasbord*, a Nordic style buffet including many types of different breads, hot and cold meat selections, cheeses, vegetables, salads and fruit. I am not proud of how much I was able to eat during the 45 minute trip, but it was good value for travellers, and it was good value for me.

I passed straight through Copenhagen with a plan to stay longer on my return journey. I made it down to the port and took the ferry across the narrow waterway to Malmo in Sweden. I expect they will build a bridge one day. My first impression of Malmo was how clean and well preserved the old buildings were. How clean the streets were and how efficiently the traffic and pedestrians circulated the city.

Everyone seemed to observe all the rules, including waiting for the lights to change before crossing the road, even when there is no likelihood of a car coming.

I made my way to the Centrum just as the working day was changing to evening, and the square was beginning to become lively with young people. Amongst these young people was quite a crowd of travellers, so I edged in and asked one of them if he knew where I could crash for the night. He was a short, well built Dutch man, helpful and friendly. As the Dutch say, "When God built him they built him like a tree, but they cut him so short." He said "We've been staying at the *West End Club*, which is now disused and broken down. It's dry, but the police come most nights and move us out. Find me later and I will show you." I said "Thanks," and carried on with my strolling, much as I had in Looe all those years ago.

I met my Dutch friend and he showed me the *West End Club*, and how to get in through the window at the back. It was dry and warm. There were already as many as twenty people asleep in their lined up sleeping bags. I duly took my place at the end of the line and got a few hours of quality sleep, before the police burst in and threw us out. Actually it was very civilised and friendly and they were most concerned that we leave no possessions behind. Duchy took me to the backup spot where I spent the rest of the night, trying to sleep on cold concrete.

I hung around with Duchy for a bit, then we went to what was apparently the cheapest and best place to eat. It was quite smart and the meal was expensive, but the quantity was huge. It was in this restaurant that I met Billy Murphy and Liverpool Billy. As we were eating we joined in conversation with two Americans at the next table, the Commander and Lieutenant of the destroyer in port. They were trying to get drunk on their day off and finding it difficult. Although Sweden is in the *Vodka Belt,* the government controls all sales of alcohol, and they have severely limited where and how much is drunk.

This relates to all the problems the country suffers every Autumn, when the Swedes go into the *Tunnel.* The light fades and it gets cold, sometimes too cold to go outside for days.

That is when the trouble starts, with crimes of rape, domestic violence, paedophilia and murder, often fuelled by alcohol, drugs and boredom. In fact Sweden has the highest crime rate in Northern Europe. We were able to help our American friends, by offering them our drinks quota that we were able to purchase when eating a meal. After a few drinks we were best of friends and the Commander offered us a tour of his ship tomorrow, which we were happy to accept.

The eating and drinking continued a while longer, when we were joined at our table by Helga. Helga was a German nurse on a break from her crushingly demanding job in an emergency ward of a hospital in Stuttgart. She was looking for a change of lifestyle and was hoping to find some fun and adventure in Sweden. Oh yes, and she was a stunner. For some reason she had taken to me and asked, "Do you mind if I hang out with you for a few days?" I said "Okay," but I'm really thinking, "What! A few days must also mean a few nights. Me. Wow."

We made our way back to the Centrum, and spent the warm evening talking to other people, but mostly talking to each other. As the evening came to a close, and people started going home, we were approached by a Swedish lady in her twenties. She said, "It doesn't look like you have anywhere to stay tonight so would you like to come to my apartment? It's just over there." We accepted and crossed the square to her lovely little apartment. We had a coffee and a chat, until the lady retired to bed, leaving us with a mattress on the floor, and a heap of clean bedding.

We set the bed up and climbed in. Helga asked, "Do you mind if I remove my bra?" I said "Er, no." and we cuddled up together. The next thing I was aware of was the smell of fresh coffee and croissants. Oh no! I had spent the night with Helga, this stunning Nordic beauty, and just fallen asleep. *I Fell asleep!* Will the opportunity ever pass my way again? Will I die a virgin? How long will it take to get over this? Well, it took at least two hours to get over it. We had to go, we were meeting the two Billies and Duchy and a few others, to go on our tour of a US Warship, part of the Cold War Defence Force.

Liverpool Billy had so much charisma and humour that he often seemed to have an entourage. People seem to want to be around someone who makes you laugh a lot, and says the things you can not easily say yourself. The more people laughed, the more funny he became. Billy Murphy was different. A native of rural County Galway, he was a soft spoken, kind person that played the guitar and sang beautifully. He would sing *Wild Colonial Boy* and *A Nation Once Again,* amongst other songs.

We were met at the harbour side by the Commander and introduced to a junior rating who would be conducting us around the ship. Within minutes, Liverpool Billy had us all in stitches. The sailor that was conducting us around his ship, caught his finger on something sharp, just about drawing blood. Helena inspected the wound, and cleaned it by putting his finger in her mouth, before tying his handkerchief around it.

A few whistles had brought almost the entire crew to their action stations in the hope of just being able to look at Helga. As the tour continued sailors were falling off gun barrels, cutting themselves on galley knives and basically dropping like flies, often in a pool of blood, but always calling for Nurse. The more intelligent ones found some nearby piece of deck that needed scrubbing, or something that needed a touch of oil. Every accident received rapid medical attention from our very own triage nurse, as we received liberal portions of their ship supplies.

At the end of the tour, I came out of it clutching a 21 lb carton of bananas, which appeared to be a standard measurement for no apparent reason. Others received cigarettes and food supplies. The tour continued, with even more side splitting laughter, until we reached the Officer's Mess, where we were offered, and accepted, lunch. It was huge. Possible the largest meal I had eaten to date. Those guys eat well.

After lunch we collected our gifted supplies and set off back to the Centrum. To my enduring shame, I wandered around the place eating the bananas, dropping the skins on the pavement. Amazingly I managed to eat the whole carton full with just a little help from Helga. I never would have thought it would be possible to eat 21lb in one go, but I managed it. I believe bananas and baked potatoes can sustain human life indefinitely. Nobody challenged my act of pollution. I have often wondered how I would confront a youth, with a 21 lb carton of bananas under his arm, littering the pavement.

It was time for me to move on. I approached Helga and asked her if she would like to travel with me. She said, "That would be lovely, but I am going back to my old life and my old boyfriend in Germany." But I thought we would be pushing up daisies together. I thought it, but didn't say it. We kissed goodbye.

Billy Murphy came to me and said, "This is my first time out of Ireland and now I want to travel and see the world. You seem to have travelled a lot, so I wondered if you could tell me the good places to go?" He then got out his song book and started a list in the back. I said, "I haven't been there but Istanbul sounds good, then you could go through Turkey and Iran to Afghanistan, maybe on to India. You could come back via Syria, Jordan and Egypt then across North Africa to Morocco." "I will do that," He said,

I went up to Liverpool Billy and my other new found friends and told them I was going to split. At that time you couldn't just decide to leave for Copenhagen on the ferry at 14.20, that was far too structured. You just split. As I walked away I thought I looked cool with my Spanish boots of Spanish leather, now with a new sole, my longish hair and my damp sleeping bag. I could imagine their unasked questions: "Who is he? Where is he going? Why is his sleeping bag always damp?" In reality they probably had a different question: "How could he eat all those bananas without sharing?"

I walked all the way to the ferry terminal in time for the 14:20 to Copenhagen. They really should build a bridge! Quite a short trip but long enough to stock up on food with their buffet style lunch. Stomach full, pockets full and duffel bag full. Ready for a new country.

The Forbidden City.

Copenhagen immediately struck me as different. How and why I would find out as I spent the first few days aimlessly wandering. More pedestrian zones, more cycles, historic buildings, little space for cars. During the 1960s, as Europe rebuilds after the war, droves of transport experts, mayors, city planners and other miscellaneous experts cross the Atlantic, in pursuit of the blueprint for a modernist world. The face of much of Europe changed and the auto-mobile ruled, but Denmark was too poor to make these changes. By the time they could afford it, they had gone off the idea, having seen how other cities across Europe had the guts ripped out of them to be replaced with fantastically complicated motorway junctions, strange looking office blocks and concrete homes in the sky. I expect many other European cities will regret their mad planning adventures and strive to reverse them in time.

Copenhagen seemed to be leading the way for humans on foot. Already they had the Stroget, the longest pedestrian-only street in the world, and some lovely smaller streets. It was in one of them, Mikkel Bryggers Gade, that I first met Eva and her boyfriend Finn. I was drinking coffee in a busy cafe, near Grand Teatret, when Eva and Finn asked if they could join me as no other seats were available. I agreed and we soon struck up a friendship. Eva had come to Denmark with her mother and elder brother, as a child refugee from Hungary, I assume after the 1956 uprising. Her brother, Ferko, worked at Tuborg but I have no idea what Eva did, and I didn't think to ask.

Eva said, "We are planning to visit some friends this afternoon. Would you like to join us?" I said I would. It turned out to be a great chance to scratch the surface of this interesting city and its people. As afternoon merged into evening Eva said "Do you have anywhere to stay this evening?" I replied, "I haven't thought about it yet." She said,

"In that case, would you like to stay with my family?" I replied "Yes please," and off we went back to hers.

After speaking to her mother in Hungarian, she showed me around. It was a tiny fourth floor apartment in Borups Alle. A tiny kitchen and shower room, a small bedroom and a larger sitting room, come bedroom. Everything was meticulously planned so every inch of space was used. The bedtime procedure involved converting the sitting room into a three-person bedroom by moving furniture around, pulling levers on the sofa, setting up beds on the floor and finding bedding in unexpected places.

The next morning we went to *Pusher Street* on the Island of Amager, so Eva could buy some cannabis resin. Like all her friends she was a regular user. This Island of Amager was mostly covered with a disused military base. Already there were signs of squatters in the old barracks. People had started building their own houses out of reclaimed building material. There was even a bike shop, and they had their own flag. The area was already known as *The Forbidden City of the Military,* although it was more commonly known as *Christiania*. I suspect it may become a famous place one day, or be closed by the authorities.

I spent several days with Eva and Finn, getting to know more of the city and its wonderful beach. Eva was an extremely social person, and through her, I met lots of interesting and exciting people. This could have gone on a lot longer, had it not been for a knock at her front door one evening. It seems one of the neighbours had contacted the police, to advise them that a long-haired foreign bloke was staying in the apartment, and he had no money.

When Eva let the policeman in, he asked to interview me in private. The first question he asked me was, "Do you have any money?" I replied, "No." He said, "It is illegal to be in Denmark with no money, so we will be sending you home. Do you agree to be sent home?" Did I have a choice? I don't know. In any event Eva's mother was getting very anxious and concerned that she had taken a step on the wrong side of the law. Perhaps she was still waiting for her Danish citizenship. I said to the policeman, "I will comply with everything, but please speak to Mrs. Kuna and explain she is not in any trouble." He spoke to her in a very kind manner and she was okay again.

It was arranged that I would be collected by a policeman, early in the morning, and escorted on to the ferry at Esbjerg on the west coast of the Jutland Peninsula. The young policeman arrived at the appointed time, I said my goodbyes and was escorted to the train station. He bought two tickets and we ascended the train for the five hour journey. Could be much shorter if they learnt how to build bridges. The policeman and I soon were on friendly terms. He was in his mid-twenties. so only perhaps seven years older than I. We talked about, well, just about everything and I will always remember it as a pleasant journey.

While waiting for the ferry link at *Middelfart*, which translates to Middle Passage in English, we stopped for lunch. It was a nice restaurant full of young trendy people. They had a very unique and odd fashion style. The boys wore brown-leather *brogues, Harris-tweed* jackets, *Oxford bags, pork-pie* hats, and they all smoked *standard Canadian pipes*. In fact they dressed almost exactly like my Dad did. Very strange.

At Esbjerg he escorted me onto the ship, gave me an allowance from the government to cover meals and any onward fares, then we said goodbye. As I sailed away I thought "Nice place, Denmark. Nice people too. I hope I didn't leave a bad impression." Suddenly I realised I was on a ship and I had no idea where it was going. I soon found out it was Harwich, a place I had never heard of, but it was in England.

A School Girl.

I arrived back in Henley-on-Thames with no money, no job, no girlfriend and no car. Still I was happy, contented, full of self confidence and sure I would be able to find a job. The very next day I found a job, working for a local family run coach company. My first task in this job was to help take bookings for a Sunday coach trip to visit the recently opened

Severn Bridge. This was a follow up from their hugely successful coach tour of the Gravelly Hill Interchange, now universally known as *Spaghetti Junction*. This job was not for me, so I left after three weeks.

Quite a short and pointless career in the coaching world. Maybe it's time for me to follow in my father's footsteps and become an engineer. I had a good look around and got an interview for a job with a well known local bearing manufacturer. I passed the interview with flying colours and started work the following day on the 6-2 shift.

It was a huge, satanic factory that generated a large amount of noise and pollution. Nobody seemed to know what they were making and why. In fact they only manufactured the cage for the ball bearings rather than the whole thing. The undemanding job involved placing a waxed card divider, in the carton, as the bearing cages were packed. A job that could easily be done faster by a well trained octopus, but the money was good so I persevered.

I still had my Lambretta scooter, which gave me freedom on the weekends. On this particular weekend I decided to travel to Castle Donington to see some of the friends I had made in Looe whilst we were on holiday. Unfortunately, half way through the weekend, the bolts sheared on the front wheel and it fell off. I phoned my boss and explained the situation and searched for someone to fix it. Eventually I found a mechanic that could fix it, but not for a week, so I had to leave it with him and hitch home.

A week later I phoned him to confirm it was ready and hitched up to collect it. The weather took a turn for the worst with heavy snow falling. I paid and left immediately to try and beat the worst of the weather. As soon as I got on the M1 Motorway the weather went downhill fast, and it turned into a snow blizzard. There was only one lane of the motorway open with few vehicles on it. After some time the blinding-snow, shivering cold and with intense-pain in my hands as they grip the handlebars, I was forced to stop under a bridge.

I began to feel a little better, but I still could not go on. I decided there was nothing to lose by trying to hitch a lift, obviously with a truck or van. Unbelievable within five minutes a large box van stopped. The driver got out and laid a plank to the back of his van, so we could push the scooter in. He gave me a lift to the nearest service station, where I was able to dry out, have a bowl of hot soup and, eventually, stop shivering. When I felt better I approached the truck drivers explaining what I wanted. It didn't take long to find one that was going as far as Slough, with an empty truck.

I gave him a packet of cigarettes to show my appreciation, we loaded the scooter and set off. When we got to Slough the weather was completely different, the snow had changed to drizzle, so I could just continue the journey under my own steam. What I hadn't realised at the time was that I had actually hitch hiked from the Midlands with a Lambretta scooter. I knew no one else that had ever done that. Perhaps, one day, I will hitchhike around Ireland with a fridge, and write a book about it.

On my way back from work, whilst walking up the hill, I passed an attractive, dark, intriguing looking school girl. The next day I passed her again, only this time we spoke. On the third occasion I said, "Do you want to come to the Yellow Submarine for a coffee?" She said "Yes. My name is Katie." I waited at the end of her road for her to change out of her school uniform. I arranged to meet her outside school again tomorrow, and before long we were seeing each other most days. Our social life together began to take shape. We went everywhere together, but mostly seemed to end up in the pub, or with a crowd of friends enjoying a smoke and a bottle of *Spanish Sauternes* in the woods around a campfire. I met her friends and she met mine, and we made new friends together.

When my parents went away for a protracted period and left us to our own devices, I thought I would steal one of their cars for the night. It went well so I made a bit of a habit out of it, sometimes taking my Mum's and sometimes my Dad's car. This backfired horribly when I decided it was time to succumb to pressure, and introduce my parents to Katie's parents. After

I had given a formal introduction Katie's Dad, Harry, said "Did you come in your Fiat or your Ford tonight?"

It got worse. I had always thought my background was far too dull. Born in South London from parents, who were also born in South London, and brought up in Surrey. I edited the story a little, to: *My Mum was looking for adventure and my Dad was starting out in a new life, and a new career, building a massive dam structure in Australia. They met on the ship going down to Australia and fell in love. I was born in Australia where they were married.* This all fell to pieces when they found out I had an older brother. I should have thought it through better.

With that out of the way we set about having fun. It was party time in our lives. A Martian looking down would wonder why we were setting out to destroy our bodies with drink, drugs, smoking, late or missing nights, loud music, poor food and mad driving. Like most of my peers it was inconceivable that I would live past the age of 30. Who the hell wanted to be 40 anyway? Probably someone who was 39 I suppose.

We were always a bit behind the USA so 1967 was the *Summer of Love UK* and the age of enlightenment. My enlightenment came on the banks of the River Thames, in the Stewards Enclosure, just after the last day of the famous Henley Royal Regatta with my trusted guide and friend Nigel, always there to show me the way. I had heard about Dr. Timothy and Gentleman Howard. I had read bits of *The Whole Earth Catalogue* and Aldous Huxley's *Doors of Perception,* I had cast the Yarrow Stalks of the *I Ching* and I was ready for a step into the unknown. Such a small thing, not much bigger than a full stop. Just a door key really, leading into my own magnificent and colossal world that had been hidden from me but could never be hidden again.

Nigel became my teacher, the one I never had at school. My education had started. I learnt to understand the beauty of *Under Milk Wood* by Dylan Thomas; the fun of *The Gingerbread Man* by J. P. Donleavy; how great generals like Stonewall Jackson could almost turn the tide against impossible odds for a deeply immoral cause; how the most shameful adventures of The Empire could spawn the beautiful works of Dominic Behan, Clancy Brothers and The Chieftains; what an Omniscient is, and how one named Kircher was lowered into the smoking crater of Mt. Vesuvius to observe how a volcano works; the wonders of Shakespeare and the health benefits of a pint of Guinness.

I learnt about the extraordinary fifth century BC, and how Socrates, Buddha and Confucius, possibly the most important philosophers of all time, were all born within ten years of each other, in completely different parts of the planet. I have further developed my own theory that they were all dyslexic, since none of them apparently ever wrote anything down. I believe dyslexia creates a powerful and immense curiosity, when one is unable to gain information from reading.

At work the next day, it suddenly struck me that I had not been to Morocco. I had been within 9 miles of Morocco, on Gibraltar, but I had not been to Morocco and I really wanted to go there, for no apparent reason. That evening I asked Katie, "Would you like to come travelling with me? We could hitch through France and Spain and across to Morocco then down to Marrakech. If hitch-hiking is not possible in Morocco, we could catch the Marrakesh Express." Now *that* would make a good song title. She said, "Yes, but I'll have to ask my Dad first." We asked him together, he talked for some time about his own experiences as a young man in the *Forgotten Army* in Burma, then he said yes.

Katie finished her exams and finished school, as she had previously planned. I continued working until we had saved enough money to set off. I made a visit to the Army & Navy Surplus store, and bought a new kit bag, and had the heels replaced on my Spanish boots of Spanish leather. There was still a limit on how much one could take out of the country, but there were two of us now and the laws were being widely flouted by this time anyway. We were ready.

City Of Bridges.

The hitch-hiking was so much easier with a girl. Our first lift was with a middle aged couple in a Citroen Safari, that's the one that has the suspension that pumps up when you put the key in the ignition. After a while we thought they were probably having an assignation. We drove through the evening and stopped in a lovely little town, where the man seemed to own, or at least have access to, a lovely little apartment. In no time the wine was out, the fire lit and dinner was on. We had a wonderful evening with much food, wine and laughter. In the morning though, she was very quiet and he was in a foul mood. Clearly something didn't go as he intended.

Our next lift left us stranded on the edge of a pine forest, in the freezing cold of night. Without delay, we walked into the forest to set up our tent. We got the tent up quickly but it was so cold we decided to light a fire. We spent over an hour trying, but failing to get one going. We collected twigs and fallen branches and used what paper we had to get a fire started, as we got colder and colder. We were even forced to use some of Katie's beautiful sketches and drawings, but still no success. Finally we took to our sleeping bag, to try to generate some warmth, swigging on a bottle of red wine until it too froze.

By the middle of the night I had run out of ideas and felt I was losing mental function and becoming sluggish and drowsy. Something was telling me to get out of this forest fast on pain of death. We roughly bundled our stuff up and limped towards the deserted road. Fortunately we did not have to wait too long before we were picked up by a van, unfortunately one without a heater. We were dropped at a cafe just as dawn was facing down the cold night. The owner lit a fire and gave us mugs of hot coffee and croissants as we enjoyed the pure pleasure of warmth and survival. I would never really know how close we were to death.

We sailed through the rest of France and Spain without a hitch, which means we were able to hitch lifts easily. It was going so well we didn't want to stop, even to rest, until the lifts dried up. Finally we arrived in Valencia, checked into a cheap hotel and collapsed on the bed, completely exhausted. We slept for a solid 18 hours and awoke starving. The restaurant below the hotel was the first place we came to, so we ordered what turned out to be a slab of meat the size of the plate it was sitting on. Since it was such good value we went for a repeat the next day. While placing the order, Katie took out a large denomination Spanish bank note to look at the picture on it. The waiter cut the slab of meat in half and tried to charge us double. When I objected he called the police and I had to pay double.

The border between La Linea was again closed to vehicles, so we had to do the last bit on foot. We passed quite quickly through Gibraltar, catching the first available ferry to Morocco, a journey of about ninety minutes. We started to hitch as soon as we disembarked, and immediately got a lift to Tetouan. This amazing place started life as a Mauritanian Berber trading town around 280 BC, before becoming a Phoenician trading port. Eventually a Roman City was founded by Augustus.

By the early 1400s, the Castilians had destroyed the city, as punishment for endless pirate raids. It was not until the end of the century that it was rebuilt, and repopulated with Muslims and Jews, fleeing the worst excesses of Ferdinand 11 and his *War of Granada*. Tetouan, known as the *White City*, later became the capital of The Spanish Protectorate of Morocco, until independence in 1956. Some buildings do look Spanish, but the only other nod to its Spanish heritage is the occasional *sombrero* worn on top of the *gallabea* hod, which looks a tad comical.

We explored the old city and happened upon what looked like a cheap hotel, so we checked in. The view from the window of the surrounding mountains was spectacular. It was here that we first laid eyes on a tall man with shoulder length hair and a beard. He said, "Hello, I am Manfred Boule from Austria. I am travelling around the Mediterranean and paying for it by displaying my paintings." There were very few like minded travellers in North Africa at the time, most having taken the road to India, so we were pleased to have someone to talk to and exchange intelligence on Morocco.

Our next stop was El Jabha, which is a pretty little port town on the edge of the Rif Mountains. It had a lovely little old town with its white houses and blue painted window frames. Apparently, blue is believed to deter flies, and I can confirm it does work. Again we managed to find the cheap place where fellow travellers stayed and we did meet fellow travellers. This is the first time we met Michele, he had changed his name from Acwulf to a more romantic sounding one, and Wilhelm Brant, both German.

Michele asked, "Where are you heading?" I said, "We are going to Marrakesh first, then further south to Tan Tan. Now I knew nothing about Tan Tan but in my mind I had linked it to Tin Tin, the famous Belgian cartoon character, that is in fact, pronounced Tan Tan. I needed to go there to sort this out. He said "Actually you are going the wrong way." It was then that I realised my mistake. I should have turned right when we left the ferry, instead I turned left. I said "Never mind, we can always go there another time." I was once again back on the trans North Africa Roman Road they once called R3.

I asked Michele, "Have you ever met Manfred?" He said, "Yes we met him in Marrakesh. You should go there, it's a nice place." When we said our goodbyes, Wilhelm said, "We are going the same direction as you, so probably see you later." Since there is basically only one sensible road to take, I am sure we will meet again later.

Our early morning lift took us through the province of Al Hoceima and into the Rif Mountains. The driver explained that this was a traditional cannabis growing area. The unpollinated female cannabis flowers are mixed with black tobacco and smoked as *kief*, in a little pipe. It is not unusual to see a policeman smoking it on point duty, or old men sitting in a cafe smoking. In fact, driving through some Berber towns with the windows open, the smell was overpowering but most pleasant.

It was a good lift taking us as far as Berkane. Sometimes we were driving by the ocean, sometimes winding through the mountains. We eventually arrived late in the evening, after a eight hour drive, in time to check into the Hotel de la Poste.

We were now in the tribal area that was once occupied by the French. Berkane didn't look very interesting, so we had an early breakfast of coffee and croissant--refusing the orange juice as it looked like it had been watered down-- and left. We crossed into Algeria later in the day.

I had always made an effort to avoid the possible danger of local water, by opting for tea, coffee or Coca-cola. Bottled water was available in some cities but the glass bottles are heavy, and there is no telling that the providers don't just use tap water anyway. This also means avoiding ice cream, ice, and washed salad and being careful when cleaning teeth. Having said that, it is sometimes impossible, or even dangerous not to drink plenty of water, especially in hot deserts. No problems so far though.

Almost as soon as I put my thumb out, a car stopped. I was now getting used to the boundless hospitality of the Arab world. The driver of the ancient Mercedes and his passenger were returning to their home of Oran in Algeria. It was a long drive so they decided to break the journey with an overnight stay. We checked into an old French colonial hotel in a town somewhere in the mountains. They had booked a room with two double beds in it, which they insisted they were duty bound to pay for.

We arrived in Oran by late morning. The name of this second city of Algeria comes from a Berber expression, meaning place of lions and relates to the sightings of Barbary Lions. It took an historic path similar to other cities along this coast: Berber, Roman, Arab, Spanish, Ottoman, French, Vichy French, British, Arab. It is the port where the French naval fleet was based during the Second World War. In fact it still is, but now it is at the bottom of the ocean, having refused to surrender to the British in 1940, it was totally destroyed by Royal Naval shell fire.

We were a little tired, so we decided to stay here for two nights. Glad we did, because it gave us a chance to wander around the old part, and enjoy the wonderful architectural style of the Jews, Spanish, Arab, Ottoman and French. Most of these impressive colonial buildings were now in a state of sad dereliction, but it still gave a powerful feel for how it was. We stopped for a coffee at the Grande Cafe, and enjoyed a Turkish coffee, in what would have been *the* place to be seen fifty years earlier.

Just outside the cafe we met Jim, begging in the street. He had left England as a student, on a grand tour, in the mid fifties, and just never stopped travelling. His mantra was: *Open your eyes and see what you can see before they close forever*. He spent the daylight hours sitting in the street, displaying a sign written in Arabic and French. Roughly translated it said: *I am an English student travelling around the world. Please help me eat by giving me arms*. In fact he made enough to indefinitely continue his lifestyle of eternal travel. I wonder if he still is travelling.

We took up position by the road, again the first car picked us up. They were going all the way to Algiers, a distance over 250 miles. It would have been nice to stop off on the way, but the driver was keen to complete the journey during daylight hours. Nevertheless the drive was outstanding, skirting the stunning Arzew Gulf and often tracking the mountainous and verdant coast, with its pristine and undamaged beaches. Our hosts were *Pied-Noir*, meaning French people born in Algeria, so of course we stopped for lunch.

Their choice was the lovely small town of Sidi Abderrahmane. After a splendid meal we were taken on a tour of the Mausoleum, just on the edge of the town. Our host explained, "When Queen Victoria visited the Mausoleum she was given a blessing that her lineage would continue. She was then asked to light the candles. When she returned home she became pregnant and was so delighted she sent a gift of these wonderful chandeliers." I discovered that King Edward VII also visited in 1905. Why they chose this remote and insignificant place to visit remains a mystery to me.

Back on our journey and a hundred miles later, we saw Manfred standing by the roadside, and of course picked him up. He said, "I have agreed to meet Michele and Wilhelm at a cheap hotel they had heard about. It's located near the Bazaar in Kauba. Shall we go there?" We agreed, and our kind driver found the area and dropped us off.

Michele and Wilhelm were already there when we arrived. We checked into this filthy but friendly hotel, and made our way to the courtyard at the back, where there was a restaurant of sorts. As we sat down to order what looked like the safest offering on the menu, we were joined by a young Dutch couple. They had hitched from Egypt, so they were able to give us some good tips on the next leg of our journey, and vice versa. Sitting in the balmy warmth of the evening, just as the muezzins began their call to evening prayers, we were exchanging travellers tales and generally putting the world to right. I wanted it to go on forever.

What an exciting city Algiers is, especially the Bazaar area. Friendly people trading in everything it's possible to trade in. Manfred set up his paintings, with a hat alongside, and proceeded to collect enough money to pay his hotel bill. On one occasion, I spotted him surrounded by dozens of locals. He was easy to spot because he was head and shoulders above the average Algerian. Because of his long hair and huge beard people were puzzled by him and his Rasputin look. I heard one young man ask him if he was a girl. In his deep booming voice he replied, "Yes I am girl." We decided we would try to do the same, and display paintings when our money was depleted, so Katie started to paint.

After a few days in Algiers, we hit the road again. A short lift took us out of the city, where another car stopped and offered us a lift. It was a family on their way home to Constantine, after a wedding. It was some way inland, but roughly in the right direction, so we gladly accepted the lift. The distance of 250 miles was simply a beautiful drive. Our driver, who spoke passable English, was very proud of his country. He explained, "Our population of 12 million people, spread over a land mass more than four times the size of France, had passed through a tough time, as they slowly recovered from 132 years of French ownership and extraction. It took a bloody war to finally kick the French out. Things were looking better now, with food production increasing, and talk of oil finds in the desert. Cities and towns were again lit, now the power stations had been repaired, after the retreating French stripped the copper wire from the generators, and any other materials of worth, in a bitter goodbye to their former colony."

I was not prepared for our arrival into Constantine. It is a walled city, built on a rock plateau, surrounded by a deep gorge on three sides. Our way in was by the stunning Sidi M'Cid bridge, although there were other possibilities in this *City of Bridges*. I think our driver chose one of the most surprising bridges to impress us. Called the *City of Bridges* because there are eight functioning bridges, and several remains of more ancient bridges and Roman Aqueducts. There are modern suspension bridges built on the site of older bridges, stone viaducts and pedestrian bridges. It's not hard to see why the Phoneticians wanted a base in this fortress Numidian city, as they set out to colonise the interior of North Africa.

As we arrived in the Royal Bazaar area of the city, the first of many muezzins had started their competing calls to evening prayer. Our host said, "Our religion dictates that if we are returning home after the start of evening prayer, it is our responsibility to offer food and refuge for the night to fellow travellers." We accepted their kind invitation and enjoyed a simple meal and a comfortable night's sleep, in a proper double bed. When we came down in the morning, we were touched to see that they were sleeping on the kitchen floor, having surrendered their bed to their guests.

After some time, really not enough time, exploring Constantine, we moved on. We had to wait for six cars to pass before we were offered a lift. Although a couple of vehicles did stop to explain they were on a very local journey, and very sorry they were not able to take us. Our next lift was driven by a French *Pied-Noir,* and he explained he could give us a lift to Philippville, but it would involve a long day driving around the mountain tribal villages, as he sold his pharmaceuticals to the medical centres. We were glad to accept and he was glad to have company.

An hour out of Constantine, I came to the view that Algeria was the most hospitable, most interesting and most beautiful country I had the pleasure of ever visiting. We saw snow capped mountains, gentle rolling hills, verdant valleys, forests, plains, orange groves and tobacco plantations, fast flowing rivers, waterfalls, lakes and salt marshes, sandy beaches and small coves. The only thing we expected to see but didn't was desert, which was slightly further south. We drove past deserted towns that once formed part of the ancient Berber Kingdom of Numidia; the Hellenistic amphitheatre of Juba II and his wife Cleopatra; Roman bridges; aqueducts and arches; Arabic madrasah and hammam; modernistic French colonial renditions of churches; post offices and opera houses. We saw poor subsistence villages, heaving market towns and modern cities, all to the sound track of evocative Arabic music. Algeria seemed to have it all, poised to become a key food producer and tourist hotspot, five years after independence.

Our driver, Terrance, took us to places where Europeans do not usually go. We travelled to the Amazigh (meaning free people), a tribal area in the foothills of the Tell Atlas Mountains. The Romans called them Berber, which means barbarian, a name given to any people that do not speak Latin. The women were very attractive, with their light skin, dark almond shaped eyes, and often wearing headdresses and elaborate traditional clothing and jewellery. A symbol of femininity, combined with stubborn resilience they can, often have, quickly morphed into fearsome resistance fighters, once giving the Busdals a bloody nose.

One particular village of large round mud huts, was a hive of activity, with the womenfolk making their pottery. Terrance explained that the method they were using was learnt from the Romans, and had not changed since then. Of course they had never seen anyone like us before, so every child in the village gathered around us to stand and stare. The staring became touching, then prodding and pulling. They were like flies around a jam pot. I had not experienced this before, and didn't know how to handle it. I started chasing them around. The poor children were running in all directions terrified. Not something I'm proud of.

Terrance completed his visit to the medical centre, so we moved on to the next village, as he continued his monthly round. As the light began to fade, and the Fennecs foxes came out to play, we made our way down the mountains towards

Phillipsville. This was the end of Terrance's round, and where we will be spending the night. Terrance was a regular visitor to Phillipsville, and was happy to share his knowledge that the Hotel above the Grand Cafe de Foy, was the only French hotel that he had faith in.

We checked into what used to be a lovely old colonial hotel, and went to our room. I immediately complained to the man on reception, "There is hardly any roof above our room." He said, "We do not think it will rain tonight. If you want, I can upgrade you to a deluxe room, but the cost will be 70 dina." Since 70 dina amounted to around 2/6, I agreed.

We were shown to another room, this time with a whole roof. No point in hanging around the room, since there was only candle light and no water, so we made our way to the Grande Cafe de Foy on the ground floor, to meet Terence. There we enjoyed a strong Arabic coffee, made by the receptionist, squatting on the floor fanning his charcoal fire.

Terrance took us out to dinner in a restaurant, on the edge of the Corniche. It was a warm evening so we sat outside. As we tucked into our assorted unknown fish, followed by mixed non-descriptive lumps of meat, washed down with excellent local red wine, and accompanied by French baguette, Terrance started to talk about his life before independence. "When Phillipsville was French the whole bay was alive. There were dozens of good restaurants, cafes, bars and dance halls." It became like some kind of orgasm of sadness, as he went on, "music, people dancing, beautiful French ladies, high class fashion houses, croissants." Tears were running down his cheeks, "One day they all left and everything went dark." I thought but didn't say, "Isn't that because you took all the copper wire from the generators?"

Money Change/Life Change.

We said our goodbyes to Terrance, and set out on the last leg of our trip across Algeria, to cross the frontier into Tunisia, at a place called Tabarka, a distance of less than 140 miles. A journey so simple it was like a day off. Not a bit of it, it was a nightmare from the off. Our first lift took us just seven miles, and the driver was a hustler. Then there were no vehicles at all, and no where to eat. Finally it started to pour with rain. It took a further six hours to complete the journey and cross the frontier into Tunisia.

We trudged into Tabarka sodden, tired and depressed. Since we had long abandoned our tent, Katie said, "I need a hotel tonight or I'll go mad." We soon found the only hotel in town, but the price was excessive. They were clearly taking advantage by requesting so much money. They wanted nearly the same as we had paid for our whole time in Algeria, for just one night's stay. It would have left us having to cut short our whole journey, so we both agreed to look for a dry place to sleep outside.

We thought this came by way of a bridge over the river, but soon after bedding down it started to rain heavily again. The rain just came through the slats and soaked us. We were forced to return to the hotel, cap in hand, and pay their inflated prices for an even shorter night. In the morning, I reluctantly paid what was due, and stole a towel, so we could dry our hair if it rained again, and left. Next stop had to be the bank to change some pounds, since this hotel had taken all our cash that we had changed at the border yesterday.

We went to the *Banque Al-Baraka,* where I handed over a ten pound note to change. Just as I did this, the telephone rang in the back office. Since the manager was the only present member of staff, he went to answer it. I could hear him talking loudly, repeating the word *asmaa,* which I think means *I hear you,* for several minutes. On impulse I reached through the wire grill and scooped up an arm full of cash. It was coins wrapped in brown waxed paper, in the shape of a stick of rock. I loaded it into my bag and we left.

Katie said, "What the hell do we do now?" I replied, "Let's have a cup of coffee and think it over." Which basically meant, I didn't have a clue. What could we do? I said, "Going back to Algeria is not an option, neither is going south, as that would eventually take us back to Algeria. The only option is east." I asked the waiter if there was a bus going east, he said not until this afternoon. We quickly left the cafe and headed out to the road, hoping for a lucky lift, and started walking. After a little while, I could see a dust cloud in the distance indicating a vehicle. Could we be lucky and get away with it?

Sadly not, it was a police car with two armed occupants. The one in a brown leather jacket, whom I took to be the officer, ordered me to empty my bag onto the road, while the other pointed his gun at my head. This was the second time in my life I had a gun pointed at me. I decided I didn't like it one bit. Of course they immediately found the money, and took us into custody at the local police station. As it turned out, the man in the brown jacket was the commander of the station. He was a good and kindly man called Ahmet.

The first day was the most frightening, not knowing our fate, but it did get better as we got to know Ahmet. Ahmet was trying to improve his English, so we often engaged in long conversations. From time to time he would like to give us displays of his strength, for example, lifting a chair by holding just one leg. Of course we were happy to show how impressed we were. He also contacted a local Dutch man, to try and help explain the situation we were in and how to best get out of it. The Dutch man was helpful, particularly for Katie, but he made no secret of showing how disgusted he was with me. Quite right too, I was disgusted with myself.

As hours ran into days, the fear was largely replaced with boredom. One day we were visited by two high ranking officers, who had basically come to look at us. I thought it was probably the first English they had taken into custody on their patch. On day three Ahmet came into our place of confinement with a big grin on his face, saying, "I've got someone to see you." Leading in a long haired European.

I said, "No way! Billy Murphy!" He said, "Good to see you Paul. You seem to be in a bit of a pickle." I said, "Just a bit." I explained what had happened. "What have you been up to Billy?" He unslung his guitar and took out his song book from the guitar case. He showed me the list of countries he had written down, when we last met in Sweden. It read Turkey, Iran, Afghanistan, Syria, Egypt and Morocco. He said, "I've been to all these places except Morocco, which is where I am heading now. I've had an amazing time, but I'm heading home now. I've been away for ten months, and now I'm missing the old country and my old folk." Billy did what Billy always did and brightened up our day. It was really good to see him.

The next day we got news that we were to appear in court, in the regional capital called Le Kef. Fear returned. We said farewell to Ahmet, this strong, powerful, hard looking man with a heart of gold, and set off on this dreadful journey. When we arrived at the court, we were immediately separated. I was put into a holding cell. They seemed to have accepted I was the sole criminal, so Katie was free to go. The holding cell was frightening, with faeces, blood and urine covering the floor and walls.

I was allocated an English teacher from the local school, to serve as my translator. I was brought up to meet him. My first question was, "Do they follow Sharia Law?" He replied, "Sharia Law was dropped in 1956. The beggars you see without hands, would have had them cut off before that date."

I sat with him for over an hour, as he asked me questions about my life in England. Eventually a messenger called us up to the court. We were asked to stand to one side as the previous case was finished.

My translator explained, "He had robbed a market stall selling sandals and, as it was his third crime in four years, would be sentenced to twelve years in prison." I was next. The prosecution read out the charges to the three judges, sitting on their raised bench and wearing impressive wigs. At this stage another barrister stood up and asked the court if he could represent me, free of charge. That being settled, the first witness, the bank manager, was called

With the poor translation and my fear, it had all become a bit of a blur. I did pick out of it something along the lines of, "I could see he was an Englishman, so I trusted him, and he broke that trust." The next witness was called, who was the receptionist from the hotel. He held up to the judges the towel that I had stolen, but forgotten about. Oh no! How bad does that make me look? There was a fairly long exchange of questions and answers, which my translator could not keep up with.

Finally it was my chance to speak. The judge in the middle asked, "Does the defendant have anything to say?" I was really winging it now. I said, "I promise I will never commit another crime in my life. I am sorry for what I have done, and I am ashamed I had broken your trust. Tunisia is a beautiful country, so please don't make me leave it before I can see it." There was a flicker of a smile on the face of one of the judges, so I thought I might be alright.

We moved on to what I assumed was the summing up. My translator said, "For this crime you will receive 20 years hard labour." A bolt of lightning crashed through the skylight and struck me on my shoulder. My legs went weak, and I started to sway backwards and forwards. He continues, "I am sorry, I meant to say if you ever do this again in Tunisia, this is the sentence you will receive, but on this occasion you are free to go." "What!" I looked up to the judges and one was smiling broadly, so I could really believe I was free.

It is not an exaggeration to say that this day has changed my life. I had peered into the abyss, not liking what I had seen, I had taken a step back. Saved by my youth and naivety, I changed, there and then. I determined that I would never again break the trust others had put in me, which of course meant I would never again break the law. Full of shame and embarrassment, and feeling awful about what I had put Katie through, I walked out of the court a man, a free man, better still an honest free man.

Over a glass of mint tea, we discussed what I had just done. Was it bank robbery or shoplifting from a bank? Either way I had been bad. No time to dwell on it, we need to leave town while the going is good. Katie said, "There's a signpost to Tunis, let's go there?" I'm really looking forward to Tunis. Tunisia is a lovely country, bursting with friendly hospitable people, and as a bonus, it's mostly pretty clean. They seem to have gotten off a little lighter from the French withdrawal, possible because it was a *protectorate* rather than a *department*. I still wonder why they paint the bottom yard of trees and large stones white.

Donkey Business.

On arrival in Tunis we made our way to Medina, because it is usually the best area in which to find a cheap hotel. We were lucky to find the historic Dar El Medina Hotel, buried in the heart of Medina. Evening prayers were being called and Tunisian music was being played in the cafe under the hotel. It was irresistible, we dumped our stuff in our room and went off exploring.

Medinas are usually cool places to be, and this was no exception. The alleyways and streets are very narrow, not because of lack of space, but to keep the direct sunlight to a minimum. As we walked through the markets the smells were amazing. I haven't travelled enough yet to be able to identify many of them, but I could pick out tea, coffee, charcoal, tobacco, meat, fish, leather, incense, hashish, fudge, carrots, rats, human sweat, cinnamon, orange juice, nutmeg, sage and cumin. Some items I recognized by sight, others I had never smelt or seen before.

Outside one market stool was a small brass dish, with something burning in it, something that smells wonderful. I asked the stool holder what it was. He said, "It is called *bakhoor,* and the pot it is burning in is called a *mabkhara.* First we place a disc of charcoal in the *mabkhara,* then we add some wood chips from the *agarwood* tree, followed by the fragrance of our choice. In this one I have added amber, musk, sugar and essential oils, but you can add what you wish. By itself it will smell of just leather, tobacco and honey." I asked, "Is it just used in markets?" He said, "No, most homes will burn it everyday. It will get into your clothes and make you smell good, even if you are in the hot desert."

Early next morning, we found a suitable place to display Katie's paintings. We choose somewhere on the edge of the Medina, where we will not disturb any traders. We set them up, with a tin beside us. Almost immediately, people start dropping small denomination coins in the tin. It soon becomes a continuous tinkle, as people come to look at the paintings, but mainly to stare at us. It is a very strange feeling to have people pay to look at you. It reminds me of *The Human Zoo*, when thousands of indigenous peoples were displayed alongside other animals in zoos and exhibitions, in major capital cities in Europe and USA. This went on from the 1800s until, this is really shameful, 1940.

We stayed for a few days and continued to get good results from our exhibitions, until it felt like time to move on. As we were checking out, the receptionist said, "Have you been to Carthage yet?" I said, "No. Is it a good place to visit?" He replied, "Not really, there is nothing much left above ground. After the Punic wars were won by the Romans, they were determined to make sure the Phoenician never again threatened Rome. They destroyed their city, killed all the inhabitants and ploughed their bones into the land." Won't bother visiting then.

We step out on the road to Sousse, which is about 100 miles away. Having looked at the map in the hotel lobby, it seems from here on, we will be in desert lands. It's a lovely drive, much of it along the coast. Although all of North Africa is predominantly Muslim, there are some noticeable differences. As we drive towards Sousse it is noticeable that the hijab is worn in a very loose way, often only covering the hair. Tunisia seems much cleaner, the buildings are better maintained and the people less constricted. More European in their outlook than other places I have been in North Africa. With the breathtaking coastline, Tunisia seems well placed for tourist development. I hope it doesn't happen, but it probably will.

Sousse has a walled Medina area, which is where we headed. We very quickly found a nice hotel. We had decided a treat was necessary. Somewhere to do a bit of washing, have a hot shower, and rest somewhere that was clean. It was over our normal budget but we thought we could do well with our exhibition and therefore cover the cost. We did well and collected about a kilo of small coins. The hotel bill came to about half a kilo. It took the staff so long to count I gave them a tip.

As we were walking out of town, looking for a suitable place to hitch, we could not help but notice a large number of camels, all heading in the same direction as us. We followed and soon came upon the regional camel market. There were hundreds of camels and even more people. The women were in their traditional Berber dress, making it look like a tribal gathering. Like all markets across the world there was food, drink and entertainment, as old friends met again, for the first time since the last market. It was spectacular.

One of the dealers said to me, "Trust in Allah, but tether your camel first." They were all tethered. Some in a most cruel way, by tying the back legs together, or by bending the foreleg and tying it, so the camel was obliged to hobble around on its knee joints, until they were raw. Even more horrible is the sharpened wood, pushed through the nostrils and secured to a rope, at each end. That looked really painful. One sees this type of cruelty throughout the Arab lands, but it should not be misinterpreted. The people are not cruel by nature. They really do look after their animals, being a large portion of their wealth, but they just have a different, maybe archaic, view of pain. Perhaps they just don't see, or can't afford the luxury of seeing what they do as cruel.

Heading towards Sfax we pass through El Jem, which is the location of the best preserved Roman amphitheatre in North Africa, better even than Rome. Although I have been here before, the first sight of this huge, elegant building is just as surprising. I noticed there was now a ticket office and a couple of cafes that were not here the last time I visited. I could say I kept it a secret, so Katie would be as surprised as I was, but in truth I had thought it was in Algeria. I really must try to buy a map.

Sfax seemed to be quite industrialised on the outskirts, but had a wonderful walled kasbah within Medina. It looked and felt more affluent than other Tunisian cities, and this was borne out by our success on our street art display. Still coins, no sign of any notes yet. I had thought our friends were in front of us and I thought it possible that we might meet here but this proved not to be the case. I wonder if we will ever meet up again? We have gone for weeks without seeing another young European to swap information and tales with, probably because they have all gone to India.

The next stop is Gabes, which is an oasis town on the coast. One is very aware of its oasis pretty much as soon as one arrives. Even more palm trees, large green areas of parkland and market gardens. We enjoyed it, especially as people were telling us there was nothing but sand for the next 1500 miles. I had been in the desert before and I loved it. Apparently I am not the first Englishman to love the desert. The Arabs are somewhat bemused by this since they love green fields, trees and water. It's a long way to go so we had better be on our way.

We arrived at the border town of Ra's Ajdir, and crossed into no man's land without any issues. The border police did give us the heads up that things were getting tricky on the Libyan side, with talk of uprisings and military coups. When we got to the Libyan side, the border police took time in studying our passport before denying us entry. I tried everything to persuade them, alas without success. As a last ditch attempt, I showed them my *Automobile Association International Driving Licence,* which did the trick. It has a photo, but I think it's the Arabic wording that did it for us, even though they were almost definitely illiterate. They never questioned Katie, probably because she was my woman.

There are far fewer cars in Libya compared with Tunisia. You really do have to go with the flow, accepting any lift going in roughly the right direction. Otherwise this enormous journey will go on forever. Travelling like this means that you do miss things, but there is no shortage of stuff to see. Actually that's not true. Just about the only stuff to see is sand, and the occasional ruined Roman town. We had one huge lift, where the driver was offering to take us all the way to Sirte. We accepted the offer but it did mean skipping Tripoli.

The one-time Italian city of Sirte had a definite edge to it, a sort of political hot-bed. It was quite noticeable in the people, who seemed under stress. The hotel manager told us that King Idris is hanging on by his fingernails, and that a young colonel in the army was plotting a coup. We decided to stay just one night, and try an exhibition in the morning, which was a good success. My arm started to ache as I plucked the Libyan Pounds that were offered us, never coins now. Women were the greatest givers, as they poked their arm from under their clothing and offered their contributions. Sometimes you could just catch sight of one, only ever one, dark brown eye, peering through their white hijab.

Just as we were approaching a good place to hitch, a small van stopped, and asked if we would like a lift, which of course we gladly accepted. He said, "My name is Francesco. I have been to the market in Sirte, to sell my produce and buy more supplies." I said, "You sound Italian." He said, "My father came here in 1912, just after the war with the Ottomans. I was born here. Actually, I learnt English from the English Army soldiers, when they occupied Libya during the war." I asked, "Was it good here, when it was ruled by your people?" He replied, "We did bad things here. By the end of Mussolini's *Pacificazione,* there were only 825,000 Libyans left alive. This is far less than the ancient population of Leptis Magna and the other great Roman cities added together. So no, it was not good."

We slowly bumped along the road, built by the Italians and now in sad disrepair. The Italians could always build good roads. We would pass the occasional Roman ruin, Mosque, farm or dusty village, with Francesco making the odd comment. As we were nearing his farm he asked, "Tonight you will eat with us, please?" I replied, "Yes please, we would like that." By the time we arrived at his farm, it was dark. His wife greeted us at the door, and we were invited to sit by the little wood stove in the gloomy candlelight. Francesco explained he had a small olive plantation that was planted by his father. He said, "It never produced a living, until we sank a well, in 1947. Now it is like an oasis in the desert, and I am proud of it."

Over a classic Italian meal and some lovely local red wine, we talked some more. He said, "We could never have any children, so when we die, the farm will disappear, become sand again, and we will be forgotten. Still this is our home, and we love it here." I thought, "Why? It's nothing but sand." Strange to see *pied-noir* in such reduced circumstances. We were offered a thin mattress to lay by the fire, and share with their black dog. We both had one of those night's sleep that are enjoyed, but apparently never appreciated, by young people.

Since Francesco's farm was on the main road, we only had to walk out the door to start hitching. Our first lift dropped us at the village Bin Jawad, which is a coastal desert village. After standing around for a long time, waiting for vehicles, we decided to walk out of town. At least we would get some respite from the crowds of curious children, and the endless, *Are you Beatle?* calls. After an hour or so standing around, we saw a dormmobile approaching in a cloud of dust. As it got closer we could clearly see that it had a British number plate. Very surprising.

It stopped and Manfred leapt out of the sliding side door. He said, "Paul, Katie, good to see you. Get in, we are going to Benghazi." Once inside, we were very happy to see Michele and Wilhelm sitting on the bench seat. The five of us were reunited again. The driver, David, was in the RAF, based just outside Benghazi. He had bought his vehicle in England and driven it down through Spain, more of less on the same route as us. The idea was to sell it in Libya and make a huge profit, but it had not gone well. He had been broken into twice and had bits of the vehicle stolen, but he was nearly there now.

We drove until nightfall and slept the night in the vehicle. In the morning, we continued. Hour after hour of desert, with nothing to see except sand, sky and the occasional line of camels, soon lost me in my own thoughts. At one point Wilhelm said, "I've just seen half a camel in a sitting position." Nobody responded. He continued, "Doesn't anyone else find that strange?" "Not really. Probably just trod on a mine," Katie replied. Some hours later there was an unwanted diversion, in the form of a loud clanking noise, followed by a hissing of steam and a hissing from David. We ground to a halt.

What to do? We really were in the middle of the desert, with nothing except sand on all horizons, and little in the way of supplies of food and water. It was a very strange feeling of helplessness, as we all struggled to come up with some kind of a plan. After an hour or so, Michele spotted a dot on the horizon. Half an hour later, it could be identified as a human. A further thirty minutes and he could be identified as a man carrying something, walking towards us. When he finally arrived, he offered us his wares, which comprised: petrol, water, a fan belt, some other car parts and some bread. We bought what we could, but unfortunately, the car parts were not helpful, so we remained stranded but now refreshed.

Half a day went by and no vehicles passed. Eventually an empty cement truck stopped, and allowed us to jump in the back. We had agreed with David, we would try to get to Benghazi and phone some of his RAF chums at his base, so they could effect a rescue. It was a horrible journey, with the wind wiping up the loose remnants of the cement in the back of the truck, and mixing with the sand. Just when we thought it could not get any worse, it poured with rain. Wilhelm said "That makes concrete, doesn't it?" We arrived at Benghazi in a filthy, tired and depressed state.

First stop was for coffee, food and to make the promised phone call for David. Second stop was the public baths. This was not a hammam, but a public bath and wash-house. Much like the ones that were all over England, in Victorian times, for the cleanliness of the labouring-class. We needed to get this sand and cement off us before it set. For a small fee, we had thirty minutes of blissful, limitless hot-water followed by clean towels and freshly-squeezed orange juice. Within half an hour, five dirty, tired and depressed young people were transformed.

We hung out having fun together for a few days in Benghazi, then went our own ways. It could be much more difficult for two men to get a lift so Michele, Wilhelm and Manfred set off separately. As we said goodbye, we all felt we would meet again soon, it always seemed to happen. Katie and I soon bagged a good lift that will take us the 360 miles to El Salloum, on the Egyptian border. We had been warned that the border was very quiet, since the breakdown of the special union that Egypt and Libya once had, called The Arab Republic of Libya and Egypt. They were right, it was completely dead. A one-horse town , or to be more accurate, a one-horse and 37 donkey town.

We quickly got to know the two border guards, who were probably pleased to have some company at this, one of the loneliest border posts in the country. Ahmet, the younger guard said, "You are welcome to build a makeshift camp here, if you want to. You don't have to worry about missing a lift, because one of our boys will ring this bell if a car approaches." We thanked him and set about making some kind of cover, to keep the sun out during the day, and protect us from the cold desert dew at night.

The very next day, Michele arrived in a water-bowser, delivering to the village on the Libyan side. We settled into a hum-drum existence, and started to develop routines. The evening routine would be triggered by the call to prayer, when we would stroll along the empty beach. Then into the village for a cup of mint tea at the makeshift cafe, before joining the locals after their prayers. Everyone would traipse up to the donkey's sand enclosure, where they would watch them mate. When the male was ready, there would be gasps from the women. After a successful event the braying donkey would be accompanied by a cheering crowd.

About day five, Manfred and Wilhelm arrived, with the two-weekly shift change of the Libyan border guards. Being all together was much more fun, but still the bell never rang. I started to wonder if anyone would ever cross this border again. Apparently, two weeks without a car is not unknown. We couldn't walk; we couldn't go back; there were no buses; we could only wait. The days became a week, then ten days, still nothing. Finally the bell rang and we all came scurrying from across the area in excited anticipation. It was a Volkswagen camper, with an international German export number plate, being driven by a Japanese-American man, accompanied by his wife.

Katie said, "We are really stuck here. We have been here for nearly two weeks. Can you please take us to the nearest town?" The driver replied, "I am really sorry but we have had a problem with hitchhikers in the States, so we vowed never to pick them up again." Katie said, "But this is a different situation. What if we give you our passports to hold as security?" He replied, "I am sorry, but no." We could hardly believe our ears, but back to the old routine it was.

The following day, Ahmet announced that he had a family problem, and had to urgently return home. His brother was collecting him, and could take us all as well. Ahmet's home town was only 60 miles down the road, but at least there was the chance of occasional cars. We made arrangements with the others, to share a room in Hotel Miramar in Alexandria, and set off on our separate journeys. The distance of just under 300 miles took us two days. The hotel, which was recommended by a French man we met in Benghazi, was better than expected, being located right on the Corniche.

We had booked the largest double room available, so when the others arrived there was plenty of room for them to sleep on the floor. We strung a washing line in the room, and set about doing our much needed washing. The next day we tried another exhibition of Katie's paintings, but it was a miserable failure. After a couple of days we all split up, again but made plans to meet again in the Milk Bar in Plaka, Athens, which was apparently where all the travellers met. We headed off to Cairo.

A Night At The Opera.

Just on the approach to Cairo, our engaging driver turned to me, sitting in the back seat to explain something in detail. He took his eyes off the road just long enough to clip the car in front. It was only a minor ding but everyone got out, including the drivers of some cars going the other way. There was much shouting and gesticulation, until it became clear that the police should be called. Even small accidents in Egypt can result in prison, so we both began to get anxious. We decided to leave the scene and carry on to Cairo on foot. The driver was most upset that we were leaving him but it seemed too risky, as foreigners, to get involved.

Cairo is a heaving mass of more than five million people, making it the largest city in Africa, but I love it. Most of the street level comprises one never ending marketplace, with every imagined artefact for sale. A good place to sit and watch, trying to make sense of what often looks like chaos. From my cafe chair I can see a boy, whose job it is to walk up and down the animal carcasses, swinging them to stop the flies landing on them for long enough to lay their eggs. I can see a goat herder, with a flock of twenty goats, right in the city centre, foraging in the residue of yesterday's vegetable market. I hear Arabic music coming from several locations, car horns, call to prayer, market traders, selling hard now before dark, church bells, trams screeching, beggars pleading for buckshee, and my waiter demanding twice the price for our tea than a local would pay.

We check into a cheap hotel, wash and regain our energy before setting off to look for a suitable place to set up our exhibition. We happened upon the Cairo Opera House, and decided to give it a try. We really need some cash to carry on. Although it was quiet, the few people that passed were generous. A passing journalist chanced to write a story about us, and being interviewed created quite a crowd that was good for business. Then it became really quiet and we were about to leave, when we were approached by a well presented man in a European suit.

He said, "Hello, my name is Aron. I am the director of this opera house. It is a very boring opera tonight. I heard you were here, so I thought I would come and say hello." We chatted about this and that. After a while, he asked, "Have you ever been to an opera?" "No," we replied in unison. He continued, "Well tomorrow is a grand opening night; would you like to see it?" "Yes please," we replied, again in unison. We made arrangements to meet the following evening, and since there was nothing doing on the exhibition front, withdrew to our hotel room for the night.

At the appointed time, we met Aron in the lobby of the Opera House. Aron said, "The house is full, so I have decided to allocate you the Presidential Box, usually used by Gamal Nasser. He only got back into power yesterday, so *he* won't be coming." We settled down to survey the wonderful surroundings we found ourselves in. Once everyone was settled, Aron joined us and gave us a bit of context. "This is the Khedivial Opera house which is the oldest and greatest in all Africa. It was built in 1869, to celebrate the completion of *our* Suez Canal. Verdi's *Aida* was commissioned by Ismail Pasha, the Khedive of Egypt and Sudan, for the opening ceremony. Unfortunately, due to the Franco-Prussian war, the sets and costumes could not be transported from Paris in time. Rigoletto was performed instead."

Suddenly it was all beginning to come alive. I asked, "Will we see *Aida* tonight, or are you still waiting for the sets and costumes?" He replied, "Ha. Tonight you will be pleased to enjoy *Rigoletto*. It is going to be performed by an Italian company. *Rigoletto's* daughter is performed by a Welsh singer called Margaret Price. I must go now, I have other duties to perform."

The performance was colourful, spectacular, elegant, professional. We appreciated the generosity, but I just didn't get it. I spent time trying to identify the Welsh lady, and not succeeding. In fact, I didn't follow the story at all. During the interval, Aron came back and asked "How are you enjoying it so far?" "Wonderful, truly wonderful." He said, "I just popped in to see if you would like to come to the First Night party, after the performance?" Katie said, "Yes please." He said, "My friend is the chief of police for all of Cairo; he will collect you from here after the performance."

Some time after the end of the performance, a man in a light-grey crumpled suit, and with two rows of gold teeth, entered our box. He put his hand out and said, "Hello English. I am Ali, chief of police for all of Cairo. I said, "I am pleased to meet you." He said, "We can go now." We were shown down to the side entrance, where a big old American car was waiting, with the engine running. We drove off with a squeal of rubber. A combination of bald tyres and hot, smooth road-surfaces meant the slightest twitch on the steering wheel, would give out that gangster scream noise. I did start to wonder if it was all a set-up, putting us in mortal danger. My mind was put to rest, when we screamed round one corner, and the white uniformed policeman snapped himself to attention and saluted.

On arrival, we were shown into this large hall, already half full of people. Ali said, "Please meet Seth. He is my chief for the centre of Cairo, he will show you where the food is." Seth took us to the side room, with the food laid out and we chatted, as I frantically stuffed my face, with as much free food as I could handle. I asked so many questions about his job that he invited us to visit him in his office, so we fixed a time and day.

Just then, Aron arrived and said, "Come, let me introduce you to someone very important. Please meet Mr. Gamal, Minister of Arts for all of Egypt. Mr. Gamal, please meet Paul and Katie. They are two successful English artists, exhibiting their paintings throughout North Africa." Mr. Gamal said, "Very pleased to meet you. Where is your next exhibition?" I was beginning to suffer from imposter syndrome. Do I own up now, or go with the flow? I said, "Cairo Hilton." He said, "I do not have much time now, but would you like to visit me at my office on Wednesday morning?" Putting my imposter syndrome aside, I accepted.

Aron said, "Please meet Margaret Price. Madame Price, please meet two English artists, who are exhibiting throughout all of North Africa." I didn't say a lot, but Katie engaged in a long conversation with her. I overheard her say, "Singing so beautifully, they should make you a dame." Aron said, "Are you hungry?" I said, "Very." We left Katie chatting to Margaret, and went to the side room to again stuff my face.

In the morning, we discussed where we could exhibit next. I said, "Perhaps the Hilton is not such a bad idea?" Katie agreed. We found our way to the Hilton and set up in a corner of the huge reception area. I noticed a man sitting at the bar, with thick rimmed glasses, red eyes, thinning grey hair and a pipe. As our eyes met, he came over to look at our paintings, pass a few words in heavily accented English, and throw a generous amount of money in our tin. The floor manager came over and said, "Do you know who that is?". We both replied that we did not. He said "That is Monsieur Jean-Paul Sartre." I said "I had no idea." If I was being more honest I should have said "I have no idea who he is."

The next day we met Seth, the Chief of Police for all of the central of Cairo, at the appointed time. He could not have been more friendly and kind to us. He asked us to join him at his desk, which was raised two feet above floor level, in consideration of his importance, I suppose. We sat there chatting as he dispensed justice. Charge him; one last chance, Abdul; you are free to go; don't treat your wife like that again, etc. One of his officers left a jam jar on his desk which he said was the contents of someone's stomach who had been poisoned. Before we left he gave us his card and said, "If you get into any trouble in Cairo, but not murder, phone me.

We travelled to the Government office to meet Mr. Gamal, Minister of Arts for all Egypt. He was very warm and welcoming and we talked for some time. He was particularly interested in life in England and anything we might know about the Beatles. He was a huge Beatles fan. He said, "Where are you staying? When we told him, he said, "I have a friend who has an empty flat in the Centre, would you like me to telephone him?" Of course we agreed, and he organised for us to be collected by his friend in an hour.

Mr. Gamal insisted we visit the newly renovated Art Centre, and spend some time with a famous Egyptian painter and sculptor, by the name of Nour. At that point we were interrupted by a tall kindly looking Russian. He introduced himself as the Sergey, Art Attaché, but told us he was really a spy that loved art. He insisted on seeing all our paintings and agreed to buy one. He told us there is very little for a Russian spy to spend money on in Cairo.

We spent a little more time in Mr. Gamal's office, drinking tea, eating various local savoury snacks, and answering questions about the Beatles and the Queen. Both were hugely positive help in our travels and got us out of the odd tricky situation. Looking out of his fifth floor window I was amazed by the volume of junk on the roof tops. Mr. Gamal informed us he had another appointment, and that we should kindly await his friend Karim, in the reception area.

Karim was much younger than our other new acquaintances, and much trendier looking, with white jeans and a sports jacket. We introduced ourselves and he took us to his sports car, for the drive to his apartment. He explained he was an only child and that his father had made a lot of money trading, during the war. I think he saw himself as a playboy, but he was a nice chap and a lot of fun.

His apartment is in Zamalek, located between Central Cairo and Giza. He explained it is one of the best areas of the city, but he only used his apartment occasionally, as he still lived with his parents. He said, "I have to go to work now, as I have arranged to meet my architect this afternoon. I will show you how everything works before I go, and where my collection of Beatles records are." He then tossed us the keys and said, "Stay as long as you like, and when you leave, post the keys in the letterbox. Enjoy yourselves and see Cairo before it changes."

The apartment was a bit too sleazy for our taste. Too much brown leather, fake fur and gold plated fittings; but we were very pleased to be there, and grateful for the trust Karim had put in us. We were only there for a short period, before we departed for the new Art Centre on the outskirts of town. We eventually found the place after some time negotiating with trams, buses and a taxi.

When we arrived we were delighted to see that Nour was expecting us. He took us into his lovely whitewashed and very cool cell, which was a confusion of paintings, sculpture and work in progress. He asked if we would like to participate in some hashish, which he had acquired from the Gaza Strip. Not wishing to rebuff his hospitality we agreed. He explained the penalty was 30 years for possession, but he trusted us because we came from the land of the Beatles.

He explained, it was not possible to buy cigarette papers in Egypt, so he took a filter cigarette and rolled it repeatedly between his fingers, until all the tobacco was in a little neat pile on his desk. He then mixed it with his hashish, and although it looked impossible, managed to get the mixture back in the cigarette. We smoked it and got high, at which point he picked up a clarinet and played some wonderful music. We talked a little; he showed us his paintings and explained what they were about; we smoked another joint; laughed a bit; sat in silence for a while and then we left. What a calm, interesting and memorable day we had. His parting words were apparently a quotation from an Egyptian philosopher, "Keep moving forward; keep discovering; keep walking until your legs no longer work, and you can walk no more."

A Strange Happening in Omonia Square.

It was time to leave Cairo, Egypt and the Arab Lands. We needed to make our way to Athens, to meet the others in the Milk Bar, on the appointed day. The trip to Alexandria was easy enough, and booking two deck class tickets on the Greek ferry to Piraeus was not a problem this time, as we were in the gap between wars, what Egyptians have come to know as peace. The duration of the crossing was stated as 2.9 days. It was pleasant enough, if a little boring. Still a good chance to shower a lot, do all our washing and relax without being hassled by anyone.

The bustling port town of Piraeus was quite a contrast after the calm of the open sea. People are still a bit on edge, probably due to the recent coup, and the oppressive political situation. We met a French girl, who was still in a state of shock because her boyfriend had been sent to jail for 30 years for the possession of a very small amount of cannabis resin. Apparently the police were picking up travellers with long hair and forcibly shaving them, under one of their new right wing laws. Looking like the Beatles, whose music sales are banned, won't be helpful for us here.

We found the Milk Bar in Plaka, but our friends were not there, and there was no message left for us. With some time to spare we decided to ask around and see if we could rent somewhere cheap for a longer period of time, possibly a month. As luck would have it, someone behind the counter knew of a place to rent in Plaka. We viewed it with the landlord and immediately accepted his offer and paid the first week in advance. It was basically one large room with a shower and kitchen area off to the side. We parked our stuff and went back to the Milk Bar, but still no word of our friends.

The following day, they did turn up and we had a great reunion. Rather than paying for a hotel we offered them space on our floor for very little money. We also made the same offer to a Dutch couple, and the seven of us went back to the house. It was a bit cramped but better than a lot of hotels we had all stayed in, and a lot of fun, as well as being cheap. That evening we all went for a wander around Omonia Square, where we were befriended by an eccentric old man. He said he was from a rich, aristocratic family but his wealth was taken from him by the Military Government. He told us to be in the square at eight the following evening to see something we will never have seen before.

Too intriguing to miss, we made our way down to the square the following evening. We were told to look for a man selling sponges, who always wore a large sponge on his head, like a hat. We did find him, apparently he is always there. At eight o'clock a pickup pulled up and two men, dressed like butlers, offloaded a small rowing boat with tiny wheels underneath. A few minutes later a chauffeur driven car arrived, and our friendly old man, now dressed as a sailor, got out. He proceeded to row around the square, before the boat was loaded back on to the pickup and disappeared, along with the old man. We just shrugged our shoulders and went home.

The following evening, the three of us were mooching around, when we were approached by three beautiful looking girls. One of them said, "Tomorrow is my birthday and I am having a big party, would you like to come?" Manfred said, "All of us?" She said, "Of course all of you. If you give me your address I will have you collected at eight." Exciting. A party usually means food, drink and nice people.

We were collected at 7:30 and taken to this large, very posh flat. The party was already in full swing, but all the attendees were extremely well dressed, in formal evening dress. We were extremely badly dressed, in torn, dirty, smelly clothes. We were introduced to the birthday girl's older brother, who was clearly appalled at what his little sister had done, by inviting us here. After an hour or so of eating, drinking and having a laugh, the brother took us aside and offered us quite a large sum of money to: "Just please to go away." Being decent people we did of course accept his offer and left.

Our little house in Plaka became a bit of a scene, with lots of people coming, staying and going. So much so that word of this reached the landlord, so he paid us an unannounced visit. There were maybe 15 people home at the time, so he was pretty appalled when he walked in. Manfred had framed and hung one of his paintings on the wall, and when he saw this he pointed at it and said, "Did I give you permission to hang your paintings in my house?" As he pointed at it, it fell off the wall and we all went silent, as though we were trying to figure out what this meant. Nothing of course, the nail was too small. I made a mental note never to become a landlord.

He threw us out there and then, returning all the money I had paid him. We all withdrew to the Milk Bar to discuss our options. Wilhelm said, "Let's go to one of the islands. I hear Hydra is rather lovely. There are lots of artists there. It will be warm so we can sleep on the beach." That sounded like a great plan, so the five of us set off back to Piraeus to catch the ferry to Hydra.

Goodbye Friends.

Hydra was beautiful. Actually it was quite barren and rocky with gravel beaches, and many of the houses were half built as was the custom. When a son or daughter got married, and was in need of a home, the parents would simply add another storey to their home, only finishing the roof when the last issue was married. It still looked very beautiful with the polished stone pavements, little houses with their whitewashed walls, blue shutters and red tiled roofs, and of course the azure sea.

We quickly established ourselves in a corner of Mandraki beach, just by a small rundown taverna. There were a few other travellers that we got to know, and it soon became a lovely little scene. The port was about a ten minute walk, so we would often wander in, to spend the evening drinking Retsina wine, socialising, dancing and smashing saucers. I started to acquire a taste for Retsina, which is flavoured with pine needles, and has a very distinctive taste; but Katie hated it. When one had drunk enough of this cheap wine, it was socially acceptable to smash saucers on the hard stone floor, as you danced holding the handkerchief of your male dance partner, making um-par noises. Of course the cost of the saucers was added to the bill.

We started to meet quite a few people, including some of the foreign residents. One such resident was a successful French artist by the name of Marceau, who had been living on Hydra since he returned from Ethiopia some years before. He spent some time talking to me about his stay in Addis Ababa, where he was contracted by Emperor Haile Selassie to paint a huge ceiling in his main palace. He made Ethiopia seem like a magical, mystical place with lots of strange and wonderful things to see, and with kind, hospitable and interesting people to meet. I said, "I want to go there one day." He said, "If your legs still work, use them, and go where you can go." I have no idea what he was talking about, there again he was a lot older than me.

One bright sunny morning I was sitting on the Quay, by myself, when a lovely Scandinavian woman and a small blond boy, enjoying an ice cream, sat next to me. We struck up a conversation. She introduced herself as Marianne from Norway. She said, "I have been learning about Red Indian mythology, and how they became the colour they are." It was a lovely story. I asked, "How long have you lived here?" She said, "My boyfriend, Leonard, bought a tiny house here seven years ago. We have had a lovely time but now we have to go. You see, he is a poet and he has failed to make enough money for us to survive, in fact he has failed to make any money, and now he is getting depressed. It is a shame because he is a good poet. I told him he needs to put his poetry to song, then I think he can make it. We are leaving the Island in three days, off to the USA." I said, "So long Marianne," and never saw her again. I hope he does make it as a poet, or maybe a singer.

The days drifted into weeks and Wilhelm drifted back to Germany. Then Michele left, then Manfred, until we were the only ones left from our original group. Of course we had met many people by now and even befriended some of the locals. There was Georgios, a local sponge diver. Sometimes we would go off with him to another island and sleep on his boat, or just hang out in a taverna and get drunk. He was a lovely, kind man, but he needed to work a bit harder at gathering sponges, if he was ever to make a living.

We met a German who introduced himself as Wolf, although I suspect it was not his real name. He was rather boring, because he would talk endlessly about how hard he was, and the hard things he had done. How good he was at fighting, how accurate at shooting and how amazing in bed. We would try to avoid him whenever we could because of all this big talk. One morning he was sitting outside the taverna looking suicidal, so I asked he what was wrong. To my amazement he burst into tears and clung to Katie sobbing. Apparently his girlfriend had left him. All the hard talk dissipated and, from then on, he became quite a pleasant chap.

We got to know Marco, the owner of a shop selling local knitwear. One day he said, "Would you like a place to stay? I have a room on the roof of my apartment which you can have for free, if you do some cleaning and a little cooking. Are you interested?" Of course we accepted, and moved in almost immediately. Unfortunately it didn't work out so well for him because we did not know how to clean, and neither of us could cook. After one particular disgusting offering of tinned meat balls, uncooked cabbage and greasy fried potatoes he felt the need to talk to us. We accepted his criticism and said we would try to do better.

After Marco had words with us we retreated to our room to lick our wounds, before going to the Taverna for a spot of lunch. When we returned to the room, it was on fire. While laying on the bed, smoking, one of us must have set the mattress alight, and not noticing, gone out leaving it to smoulder. I managed to douse the flames, but it still left a horrible black mess. Since we were not on the best of terms with Marco, and we had lost our place to stay, we decided to leave on the afternoon ferry. Not very brave really.

We made our way to the port and waited for the ferry. Of course, a neighbour had informed Marco of the fire, so he intercepted us at the ferry. Understandably, Marco must have thought we were disgruntled, and had chosen to set fire to his house, before affecting our escape. Fortunately my duffel bag was badly burnt, so at least he could dispel that theory. I would have gladly paid to replace the mattress, and repaint the place, but we just didn't have enough money for that, and to get home, so I left, promising to pay him next time I was on the Island.

As we left on the ferry to Piraeus, we sat in silence, immersed in our own thoughts, me not really understanding why it ever had to end. Hydra has been described as like a flower opening up as you pass the headland, and pull into the port. Now it was the same in reverse; like a flower closing up. Our time on Hydra was coming to an end. We discussed our options, and very quickly decided to just go straight home, while our money held out.

We still had over 2000 miles to go, so there were still opportunities for adventure, but neither of us were interested any more. We just wanted to get home as quickly as possible, so that became our main focus. Staying on the road most of the time means often sleeping by the roadside, eating in roadside places and not often going into towns. It also meant sometimes feeling hungry, really hungry. Not because we were completely penniless, but because we were on a quiet road with nowhere to buy food. Going to sleep having not eaten anything the previous day, and waking up ravenous, is an experience I think everyone should endure, to understand how most people in the world live.

Onwards we went, up through Northern Greece, on to the E5 then into Yugoslavia. The area known as Macedonia, confusingly not the place of the same name in Greece, where Alexandria became king, was a dry and dusty place. The regional capital of Skopje was in a terrible state having suffered a serious earthquake in 1963, that destroyed 80% of the buildings and killed hundreds of people. It looked like they had hardly started the process of rebuilding, which probably explained why the population looked and sounded so miserable.

Early the following morning, we crossed into the Yugoslavian Socialist Republic of Kosovo, and Wow! We travelled through snow capped mountains and past tumbling waterfalls. The flat plains were covered in that really dark gold coloured wheat, maze and the occasional small corner of a field planted with peppermint and chamomile, presumably for tea. The local folk were small and dark, sometimes in cultural clothing, and almost always carrying a hoe or a pitchfork or something farming related.

The villages were small and rural in nature. Apparently barely more than a million people share this region, most of whom are ethnic Albanian farmers. We passed Monasteries, Orthodox churches and Mosques as well as Byzantine and Roman ruins. Our lift had taken us a bit further south, judging by the position of the rising sun. A map would be handy. We arrived in a place called Gjakove, around lunchtime. We would pad around for a bit and see who's about.

We didn't get far before we came upon the Grand Bazaar, which looked remarkably similar to other bazaars we had seen in North Africa. Hundreds of shops were selling everything from antique luxurious guns to brightly painted furniture, antique books, smoking pipes, textiles and more. The far end was for consumable organics and had the smells to go with it. We went strolling until dusk, then walked out of town to camp in the next valley in a quiet spot. It poured with rain.

By dawn the rain had slowed to a steady, continuous drizzle, and it was quite chilly. Always difficult to get out of the sleeping bag, get dressed, and pack up damp camping gear in the rain, we delayed it as long as possible. When I looked out of the tent flap I was amazed to see hundreds of curious men and women, trudging to their work in the fields, in the rain, looking more like automatons than people. No new Peasant's Farm Collectives were being created since the 1950 Cazin Peasants Revolt, but the Cooperatives didn't seem much better. The Peasants were still forced to meet quotas, regardless of weather conditions, or risk fines often leading to bankruptcy.

Dropping down from the mountains we pass the slightly boring, flat cultivated planes of the Socialist Republic of

Serbia, then through the badlands of the north of Croatia, before again climbing up to the Julian Alps of Slovenia. Leaving Slovenia to cross into Austria revealed little geographic change, but a great social difference. Yugoslavia has, and still is, a dirt poor region, only avoiding famine in the late 1940s due to USA famine relief. I cannot see the reason for it being so poor, other than a failure of their system. I am guessing it won't last much longer, especially without the ageing President Tito holding it together.

Lift wise we were on a definite roll, gobbling up the miles and countries. This came to an end when we were dropped near the centre of the small city of Ulm, famous as the birthplace of Albert Einstein, on the border of Bavaria. We calculated we could just about afford a night in a cheap hotel, if we could find one. We went from *gasthaus* to *gasthaus* with always the same negative reply, "We are full." I did not believe it.

We asked at one particular *gasthaus* and received the standard reply. I asked for a drink at the crowded bar, and they would not serve us that either. A Turkish looking man came up to us, and suggested he would be able to help, as he was a fluent German speaker and he knew the City well. We were so desperate we agreed and went off with him to receive the same reply from several more *gasthaus*, this time said with more aggression. Finally he suggested we could sleep at his place, if we didn't mind cramped conditions. We readily accepted his offer.

I wasn't feeling that happy with the situation, but I hadn't read any danger signals. We arrived at a complex of high rise flats, and as we walked through the courtyard, a Turkish woman leaned out of the window and had an altercation with him. Finally we made it to his bedsitter, which was filthy and depressing. He gave us a sandwich, and drink, and suggested we could sleep in his double bed. He would sleep somewhere else. We got ready for bed, keeping most of our clothes on, mainly because the bed looked pretty dirty.

Within minutes of getting into bed he took all his clothes off and jumped in between us. I quickly manoeuvred myself so I was between Katie and him, but frankly, I was not sure if he was interested in myself, Katie or both of us. Any charm that he had quickly disappeared as he sat up in bed, naked, smoking and behaving like a husband whose wife had just announced she had yet another headache. He became really aggressive so we fled. Feeling shaken and not wishing to hitch a lift in the middle of the night we just walked. We walked until we reached a suitable place to hitch and sat in a transport cafe until dawn.

Now even more determined to get home as soon as possible, we hardly stopped hitching and hardly slept. We gratefully accepted a lift from a truck with TIR (Transports Internationaux Routiers) plates heading for the Channel. He kindly let us sleep in his bunk while we made slow progress to the port of Calais. We steamed into Dover on a gloomy Wednesday evening, too tired to go on without a night's sleep. After a poor night's sleep in a damp sleeping bag we finally arrived in Henley-on-Thames on Thursday.

Breaking-up is Hard To Do.

We went straight to Katie's house where I was greeted by her parents. Harry said, "You brought her back home then." I said, "Back safe and sound, as I promised." Katie stayed with her parents and I walked home alone. We were separated for the first time in months. Of course we would see each other soon, but it was a very strange feeling.

Harry was a partner in a small electrical contractor company. He kindly offered me a job, which I gladly accepted. My work colleagues were a good crowd, so I thought I could get on well here. My very first job was on a large Ministry of Defence housing site. I was given the task of drilling a 3⁄4 inch hole through every joist in every house on the estate, with a bit & brace. It was hard work, especially as I didn't know how to sharpen the bit. I wish someone would invent a battery powered drill.

There was a lot of downtime, while we waited for materials, or instructions from the Clerk of the Works, who was a captain in the army. During this down time we would play three card brag and trade materials with the other tradesmen. Electricians would swap light bulbs for taps from the plumbers, bath tubs for infrared heaters, or floor tiles for 8 x 4 timber. One Friday evening, I was helping a tiler lift a steel bathtub into the back of his van, when the Clerk of the Works, who just happened to be walking past, stopped and gave us a hand. He either had no idea or he just didn't care that the goods were being stolen.

I worked there for many months and earned quite a good wage. A lot of it went in partying, drunken weekends away, and nights in the pub; but I soon managed to save enough to buy a car. I bought a very old Citroen 2CV, also known as a *Deux Chevaux*, that had been driven here by a returning traveller and registered for use in England. The annual M.O.T check had just been reduced from ten years to three, but the date ran from the date of the first registration, so I would be able to legally drive this death trap for three years before it needed a M.O.T test.

The problem driving a 2CV in England was that people were not used to them, and did not understand them as they did in France. The main issue was the small engines and the slow speed going up hills. On a long hill it would slow down to an average walking speed, and could take ten minutes to summit a long hill. Sometimes there could be a huge tailback of traffic, which was a particular problem for heavy lorries, and could delay their lunch by half an hour. The faster cars would be able to overtake at great risk of a head on crash, which is why I call it a death trap.

The driver's seat was broken, so I had secured it in place with a large steel cramp. The problem was that it jutted out in such a way that it blocked my exit from the vehicle, and had to be stepped over. Sometimes I would remember but often I wouldn't, which would result in me falling on my face, on at least one occasion, into a puddle. I would sometimes arrive home after driving around, and my face was so battered it looked like I had been in a fight.

Apart from my day job, I rented a room with Katie, for the purpose of setting up an artist studio, in the hope of selling some of Katie's paintings. I learnt how to cut mounts and frame her paintings, but it didn't work out. We never managed to sell a worthwhile number of paintings. It did however lead to my starting a picture framing business. I would work during the week and do my framing at weekends. I soon rented a workshop from a neighbour, as the business started to grow.

Katie and I were not getting on well. The relationship was not able to survive our return to civilization, and any kind of normal existence. Sadly, we agreed to separate, before we did any harm to ourselves or each other. What an adventure we had though. I had to stop working for Harry, partly because of our breakup, but also because I was fed-up with all the travelling to work and the long days. In no time, I got a new job, working for Sir George Godfrey and Partners, which gave me more time to build up my picture framing business.

Sir George Godfrey and Partners was an old WW2 aircraft-parts manufacturing company, built underground, in a redundant chalk mine, in Wargrave near Henley-on-Thames. Most of the staff worked there during the war, and one had the feeling it was only in operation now to keep them employed. I was employed as a labourer under the management of the then Mayor of Henley-on-Thames, a kind and interesting man, happy to pass on his superior knowledge of just about everything. I hated working underground and left after a few weeks.

I decided to put my little business on hold and go to Istanbul, not knowing where it was, but loving the sound of the name. I would be going with a friend, Joe, whom I had met recently, playing at a folk club in the West Country. He spoke very slowly, and had little to say, but could sing and play the guitar beautifully. We were going by train, mostly on the Orient Express. I was so looking forward to striding into the ticket office in Reading, and saying, "Single to Istanbul please." When the moment came, the ticket clerk didn't even look up from his ledger, he just said, "Fourteen pounds seven and six please."

The train journey was amazing, with all sorts of mysterious people going about their business. At the Yugoslavian border, the armed guard threw me against the partition, pointed his gun at me, and demanded I take my jacket off. Apparently my passport pouch, that my Mother had made for me all those years ago, and was still in service on my belt, looked like it could have been a gun holster.

It was great, thundering across Europe on this long train, powered by this huge steam engine. I was surprised to see that in Bulgaria, the peasants seemed to have a legal right to stop the train for a lift. It was strange to see this great train scream to a halt to pick up a few peasants, their goats and maybe a bail of straw. Finally we reached Istanbul and everyone disembarked, their secrets intact. We made our way to the Hotel Gulhane, which was known to be the cheapest hippy hotel in the City. We booked the cheapest spot, which was a place to lay our sleeping bags on the canvas-covered roof.

Many balmy evenings were spent in the Gulhane Park with the small international community of travellers and a few locals. Playing guitar, talking, playing chess and having fun. We were often joined by a Turkish man named Ali. He lived in the park, which he called his *Star Hotel*. His only possession was a sitar with a hole in the soundbox, where he would keep his scraps of food. Istanbul was a busy city, but there seemed to be many people on the starvation borderline, especially children, if they were unable to get even the poorest paid jobs. It was not unusual to see subsistence farmers bringing their goat herds into the city, to try to attain a better price.

We had an attempt to make money by Joe busking, but it didn't work out, so Joe and I went our own ways. I did, however, meet a friendly local man who spoke good English. He invited me back to his house, in the heart of the city, where he lived with his parents, Cypriot wife and their young son . His father was an advisor to the late president Mustafa Ataturk, before his death in 1938, and he proudly displayed a photograph of them both embracing. I was fed and made to feel welcome.

The matriarchal figure of the household suggested I could teach her ten year old grandson maths, in the English language. I readily accepted her offer, and we agreed I would be paid by way of a meal and taxi fare home, for three afternoons a week. I got on well with Barbour and I soon fell into a comfortable routine. I probably started to overstay my welcome, particularly from the Father's point of view. One day they had a wood stove, and a long stove pipe delivered, but being a retired university academic, he had no clue how to install it. I managed to do a superb job of the installation, and my place in the family unit was restored. However it all fell to pieces when the grandmother came to realise that I could not spell even simple words, so it ended, but in a good way. My finances exhausted I hitched home, back on the E5 for the third time in my life.

I returned to my family home, and life continued, but I was a changed person. My brother John had set off for India with a friend called Steve. Steve couldn't hack it, and returned after a few days. Nothing was heard from John for weeks and my Mother was getting more and more worried. One day, many weeks after he had left, a postcard from John arrived. She turned it over to read the words, "Everything Groovy." She said, "Well that's a damn silly thing to say." But I understood. I really wanted to go to India.

The picture framing business was doing so well, I was able to take it on as a full time occupation. I made up a board showing samples of the mouldings and mounts, and concocted a price list and hit the streets. I went from door to door asking if the householders had anything they wanted to have framed. Of course they did, everyone had a certificate, or a painting they had bought on holiday, or a family portrait that they just never got around to framing. Some areas were not good but occasionally I would find a rich seam of gold.

On one particular occasion, I found myself on a housing estate for military officers and their families. When I returned several framed items to one particular colonel's wife, she was in the middle of hosting a coffee morning. I was introduced to the other ladies as her picture framer, and I immediately found myself with lots of lucrative work. On another occasion, I was approached by a well known Czechoslovakian artist, who had been let down by another provider. He was in a panic as he had an exhibition, due to start the very next day. I promised him I could get the job done, and having no other options, he contracted me. I worked all day and all through the night, and managed to deliver his framed paintings at seven on the morning of the exhibition.

Another streak of gold was when the toothpaste company Pepsodent had an offer of a set of four prints, of landscape paintings, by the Australian artist Rolf Harris. I would guess every other house, on one particular housing estate, had this set of prints to frame. Rather amusingly, another source of my minimal wealth were impressionist paintings on black card. Each customer would give me a story about how they had the pleasure of meeting the artist when they were on holiday in Spain, yet the paintings were almost identical and clearly produced in a factory.

I was in that wonderful position of being a nineteen year old, with lots of ideas and energy, yet nothing to lose. I took a risk and opened a small artists supply shop, in Henley-on-Thames, with a view to selling supplies, and offering a picture framing service. I don't know if it was the first in Henley, but it was certainly the only one in town at the time, and it was well received. Artists came down from the mountains to buy their supplies of ultramarine, while others took up painting for the first time. I soon got bored, so I offered it to my Mother to run and she gladly accepted, although it was never a financial success.

One wet Tuesday I was thrown out of home for not keeping to the rules. I probably deserved it, and agreed it was about time, even though I didn't actually have anywhere else to live. Really, just to make a point, I slept in my car, which I parked just outside my parents architect designed house, they had built in a well to do road, just outside of town. I have to say being homeless did not bother me at all, and was probably a useful experience.

Polska Piękność.

My social life was fun, but I had no girlfriend, and as a young person, of course I really wanted to share my life with someone. One Friday night I went to Reading with two friends, and we noticed three girls waiting by a bus stop. I offered them a lift and somehow they all managed to cram into the back of my *Deux Chevaux*, reducing the top speed to a steady fifteen miles per hour. It was late and there was nowhere we could think of to go, so we dropped them off outside the house of one of them. This particular girl showed an interest in me, so I asked her if she would like to go out and she accepted.

When I went to collect her the next evening, she answered the door and invited me in. She said, "My name is Sonia by the way." Sonia introduced me to her father, who was a serious looking Polish man, who spoke good English with a heavy accent. Her Mother was a warm, friendly woman but she spoke little English, or so she claimed. Her Dad, Stanislav, was a watch and clock repairer working for British Rail during the day, and for himself at night. When I told him about my business, we immediately hit it off, and I had the feeling we would continue to do so.

I decided to look for a job in Reading, and continue picture framing in the evenings. I quickly found one working as a banana delivery driver and salesman. This meant a very early start in the morning, to deliver to all the local greengrocers. On one occasion, I decided to see if I could get a sale from a supermarket chain called Baileys, and by chance, the group fruit and vegetable buyer was present. He gave me a large order, and visited my boss to give him an ongoing contract. My boss was over the moon. No one had ever shown initiative like that, in three generations of this family business.

I continued to see Sonia at every opportunity. I was intrigued by her, and her stunning good looks. I was falling for her, no doubt. She told me she was working as a receptionist for a doctors surgery in Reading. The surgery was on the ground floor of a large, five storey Georgian house in a Georgian terrace, known as Virgins Retreat, apparently because the other properties were occupied by first year student virgins, from Reading University. Apart from the basement, where a caretaker and his family lived, and the ground floor surgery, the rest of the house was empty.

I now had a bit of money from my banana round, so I said to Sonia, "Lets bugger off to Morocco for a week or so." She agreed, so I booked two British European Airline flights to Gibraltar, which were cheap, probably because they were subsidised by the Government in order to keep Gibraltar in the fold. This was the first time Sonia had been on a plane and my second. It was December and fast approaching Christmas, so we chose to spend a few days in Gibraltar. Christmas day was a bit of a sad occasion, in a large hotel full of strangers, all trying and failing to look like they were having a great time.

I became rather unwell with some kind of lung infection. One evening, sitting on the Rock, we were passed by many sailors coming back from the casino. An older sailor, referred to as *buffer* by the passing young seamen, sat beside us and we struck up a conversation. He could see I was having a problem with my lungs. He said, "Come on board tomorrow morning and you can see the doctor. I will also show you around and you can see where your tax is spent." I had heard of this tax thing before.

The next morning I attended the doctor on board. He gave me a thorough check-up and prescribed some medication. *Buffer* met us and gave us a fascinating tour of the ship. Spain was playing up again, and had just shut the border to Gibraltar. They had also been pressing on our defences around an area of the sea called the *Hook*. Apparently they had to fire some warning shots yesterday.

From Gibraltar it was only a few minutes flying time, on the local family owned airline, to Tangier, in Morocco. We bought some tickets and were there in less than fifteen minutes. Sonia was waved through border control, but I was refused entry. They had just made some changes, and would no longer allow any foreigners to enter, if they had hair over their collar. I had to return on the same flight to get a haircut. I returned to Morocco the next day and was met by Sonia at the airport, with her new found Moroccan friend. He had done a good job keeping her safe in Tangier, probably the only dangerous city in Morocco, and home to the notorious *Black Cat Bar.*

We travelled around a small area of Morocco and spent some days in Spanish Ceuta, but my health was going downhill. I tried to rest up for a few days before the return journey, but I was not much better. Back in England the doctor soon sorted me out with a course of antibiotics. I was feeling much better in no time, and glad to be home.

Marry Me.

Sonia's boss offered her the top three floors above the surgery, rent free. She had some days of negotiating with her parents before they agreed, and she would gladly accept the offer, and move out of home for the first time. I started to visit her in her new home, and after a couple of weeks, she said I could move in. Being homeless, and still sleeping in my car, I was happy to accept. There was nothing at all in this huge apartment so we set about getting hold of what furniture we could find, including an old gas cooker. One particular night, while I was staying there, her Dad must have cycled past, and again in the morning. When I took Sonia home on Sunday, for Sunday lunch Polish style, Stanislav rushed out of the house to make a note of my car number plate. He was now able to demonstrate that I had spent the night with her.

This was actually quite a big deal for Sonia, and it also meant that he would not come and install our gas cooker. I had fallen for this Polish beauty and I wanted her forever. There was nothing else to really consider, so I said, "Will you marry me?" She said, "Okay." I have always found I make the best decisions in life if I make them quickly, and this was a good decision. The next morning I went to see her Dad, to ask if I could marry his daughter. I was met at the door by her very frosty Mother, and shown into Stanislav's workshop. He said, "What do you want now?" without looking up from his work. I said, "I want to marry your daughter." He swung around on his chair, and said, "Do you love her?" I said, "Yes." He said, "Very good, very very good. I will come and fit the cooker on Saturday."

We had to do this thing quickly, but I've no idea why. I obtained a special licence from the Reading Register Office. The marriage was to take place on Friday afternoon at two, so I had arranged to have the afternoon off work. We decided to keep it small, so we only had a couple of friends as witnesses, and no family present. Stanislav thought it a very good idea, not to waste money on a big wedding. My parents accepted it, although my Mum was convinced Sonia was pregnant which, she reasonably thought, explained the rush. In the evening some friends from Henley came over and we got drunk and I woke up a married man. We were both twenty and we had known each other for just three months.

For no apparent reason I sold my little picture framing business. I should have discussed it with my wife, but frankly I hadn't thought of it, being so used to making all my decisions alone. I made a pledge to discuss everything in the future. I sold the stock, work-in-progress, tools and goodwill. We both had no idea how to go about married life, and since none of our close friends were yet married, we had no role models. Sonia did her best at cooking, She once produced a curry that was so hot I considered hospital treatment. Our attempts at housekeeping resulted in me having to phone the Milk Vessel Recovery Service, and ask them to take away around 800 dirty milk bottles. I was hopeless at just about everything. We would have to try to learn together.

The Bus.

Sonia's job as a doctor's receptionist and assistant took a rather unpleasant turn. The junior doctor of the practice, Doctor Drinkwater, had been self medicating for years and went completely off the rails. He was forced to leave the practice, but he continued as a GP in Great Yarmouth. His final act was to murder one of his patients. It was quite shocking for us to think he had been working with Sonia, and what harm he may have done to others without her knowledge. May his soul rot in hell.

I had made some money selling my business, and topped it up by selling bananas, so we discussed a plan to buy a bus and start a bus service. I bought a Volkswagen bus that had been partially converted from a van. It had windows cut into it but little else. I parked it up at the in-laws' and started to complete the conversion. Using wooden banana boxes and copious amounts of foam rubber, obtained from a market stall, we were soon ready to roll, with a seating capacity for eight paying passengers. Next problem was where to go and how to find passengers. I had rather stupidly assumed droves of my friends would like to pay for a place, but no one came forward. We thought we would go anyway, a man, a woman, a bus, no plan.

I came up with a plan that was simple enough. To park outside a Youth Hostel or traveller's hotel in Germany, and put a sign up, offering a seat to Istanbul for £10. It seemed like a reasonable plan since there were so many people on the road to India. We planned to leave in early May 1970, but fate intervened. Sonia fell and badly broke her arm. We eventually got away in June, although Sonia's arm was still in plaster, and she was not feeling great about it. She had quit her job and passed it on to an Italian friend.

We took our time crossing Europe, stopping to visit friends and doing a bit of sightseeing. We picked up a couple of hitch-hikers in Holland who were happy to pay for the trip to Istanbul, but I needed to find six more. We decided to park up at the Munich Youth Hostel, put a sign up in the windscreen and just wait. People would come out of the Hostel first thing in the morning, try sitting on the steps, until the warden came out and threw a bucket of water over the steps to move them on, then walk past us. In less than a day, we found another six paying passengers of various nationalities, including an Alaskan student, a huge Irish bookbinder and a Canadian girl. We were off.

Finally we crossed the border from Greece to Turkey. It was a huge contrast between the cleanliness and modernity of Greece, to the dilapidated buildings and dirty streets of Turkey, although Turkey somehow seemed more welcoming. Crossing a border like this one with a vehicle is never easy.

They are always on the lookout for people selling their vehicles in Turkey, thus avoiding the high tax and making a huge profit. In the event of a crash, even the written off vehicle must be somehow transported across the border, to a huge vehicle graveyard in no man's land.

It is my birthday today. I am a married man of twenty one. I could now vote for the first time; marry without parental consent, good job I had asked Sonia's Dad first; have sex with another man in private, no point, I'm married now, although I wouldn't have wanted to do it anyway, and certainly not in public; take on a mortgage; open a credit card, only if you are a man; go to proper grown up prison, rather than borstal. I was old enough to buy a subsidised ticket to Australia and become a T*en Pound Pom;* become a *Homesteader* and pick up my free 160 acres of land, as promised to me by the Canadian Government all those years ago. It is the day that Edward Heath is elected prime minister; *Bridge over Troubled Waters* is top of the hit parade; *Little Big Man* is the best selling film. The killing in Vietnam goes on apace as fear of an atomic war is mounting.

Upon arriving at Istanbul, Irish asked if I could help him change some money on the black market and I agreed. We hailed a *dolmouch,* which is a shared taxi system often using a pre war American car; in this case it was a Pilot Superjet. Once all the other passengers had been dropped off, we asked him about changing some cash. He said, "Yes my friend, my brother's friend will help with this." We drove to a cafe and his brother's friend, also with mostly gold teeth, jumped in. We drove around the corner and stopped, to discuss the amount. Irish gave him his British Pounds and he disappeared into a market, saying he will be back in five minutes.

That was the last we saw of him, it was *that* simple. The driver said, "He will be back soon. He has never let me down before." Irish got the driver in a headlock, and he agreed to repay the money, but would have to go to his office to get it. He drove back to the taxi rank, and it dawned on us that we were in his place, and were surrounded by many of his taxi driver friends, most of whom also had gold teeth. There was nothing we could do, they had won.

Sonia and I checked into one of the cheapest hotels, called Hotel Stop, in Sultanahmet. Sultanahmet is where all the freaks and travellers stay. It has a great atmosphere and is the location of the Blue Mosque, the Greek Hagia Sophia Cathedral, Topkapi Palace, the Grand Bazaar and of course the Pudding Shop. I love the place, but it was a bit of a culture shock for Sonia. We settled into our grim, depressing, hotel room and caught up on some much needed sleep after our drive of just under 2000 miles. The big sleep continued well into the next day, until we awoke hungry, and settled for the nearest street food.

The next day I woke to a severe dose of the trots, which could have been dysentery. I was so bad I spent most of the day sitting on a drain in a *hammam*, to save rushing to the toilet every two minutes. I was drained and exhausted when it finally passed through my system. Meanwhile, Sonia was feeling so dirty she took a bath, and her plaster became so sodden she took it off and placed it under the bed. Things were not going to plan, even if we had no plan to go by. We had stayed too long and our money was already exhausted. Hotel Stop became just that. The room had bars on the window, which was probably too small to get out of anyway, and the hotel held our passport. Things needed to improve.

Exhausted.

The next morning, feeling better, we headed off to the Pudding Shop. This was a great place to hang out, with just about every nationality represented. There were people on their way to India; people on the way back; dealers looking to score and import drugs to Europe; people just stuck there. It was the place to exchange ideas; make new friends; fall in love before carrying on to Afghanistan; gain useful information about the next destination, and, of course, eat lots of their delicious puddings. In no time, I had sold six spaces for the return trip to Munich; enough to buy our passports back from the hotel, tank-up and get going.

One of our passengers was a rather loud mouth American, called Jerry, travelling by himself, which was no surprise. When we reached the Greek customs, the officer asked me if I was smuggling any drugs. I already knew they were hot on this, because of the political situation. I had heard of the long sentences they were passing out for smuggling, even the smallest amount of cannabis, so I would never have carried anything. The customs officer then took each passenger aside, and asked them the same question, "Are you in possession of any drugs?" Unbelievably, Jerry said, "Only a large amount of cannabis." as a joke.

The customs officer called two associates over, and they took the bus to a hydraulic ramp, and set to work stripping it down. They took off the side panels; door panels; investigated the engine and petrol tank, and removed the spare tyre from the wheel. While they worked on the bus, the first officer worked on me. He was actually quite pleasant, with a large hint of menace. One trick he used was to put his face three inches from mine, and ask me if I was carrying anything, while his right hand was resting on my chest, to see if my heart rate increased. Of course it increased.

Once the officer was satisfied, he said to me, "You can go now Paul. I am sorry but I had to do all that, but I had to respond to the loud American's comment. I had no choice. Have a safe journey and I wish you good luck." I had spent two stressful hours sitting in the sun, through no fault of mine, but at least Jerry had stopped talking.

Soon after crossing to Greece, I spotted a couple by the roadside, and asked them if they would like to buy a ticket to Munchen, which they readily accepted. They had no luggage other than a large Greek urn. When I questioned why they would travel with just a Greek urn, he said, "It is a symbol of our love. In the unhappy event that it breaks, our love will also break." They must be Swedish, I thought, as I happily settled down to the 1000 mile drive, with a full load.

Munich was civilization for us, the place we would sort ourselves out, eat well, sort the bus out, and tank up with clean fuel. We were sleeping in the bus, so we would not miss any potential business. Sure enough, the very first day nine English long-haired guys booked me out, one of which paid a reduced rate to sit right at the back, on the engine. They were all from the town of Heston in Middlesex. Strange, I thought, to name a town after a motorway service station.

These nine boys had been friends for most of their lives, but none of them had ever been out of the country, and had no idea what to expect with this, their first overseas adventure. They were all quite different and had diverse talents. Rob had a guitar and could do a wonderful rendition of "... and I give them both the best with natural Shredded Wheat." Nigel was the funny one who kept me laughing until my face ached. John was the planner with his map, copy of The Last Whole Earth Catalogue Ever, guide book and first aid book. There was also a moaner, a smartie and a sleeper. It was loads of fun crossing Europe with these guys.

When we arrived in Edirne in Turkey, around dusk, I parked up at the side of this deserted road. We could move some of the banana boxes around the bus, to make a double bed of sorts, but all our passengers had to sleep outside, as agreed at the start, sometimes with, sometimes without a tent. We all sat outside as the sun set and were eating, talking and smoking when the packs of wild dogs started howling from several directions, followed by the startled alarm of donkeys. They bedded down in their sleeping bags, in the shape of a phalanx, with Rob and John on first watch, with their tiny penknives, open and at the ready.

Next morning we travelled straight to Istanbul, dropped our friends and checked into the American Tourist Hotel. It was a step up from Hotel Stop, but not as grand as the name would allure to. After a long rest, I thought I would visit the manufacturing side of the Grand Bazaar, to seek out business opportunities. I saw some beautiful hand embroidered blouses that I thought might be saleable in England, and some amazing full length sheepskin coats, in different colours and designs. I thought these showed great potential, so I made a mental note to perhaps take some back.

Driving away from the manufacturing centre, we got hopelessly lost in the Grand Bazaar. This was a problem because Turkey was in a state of political turmoil, and the government had just decreed yet again, a dusk until dawn curfew, and the sun had just set. It was a bit scary driving around the maze of deserted streets, desperate to find a way out. I tried turning left at every junction, but after another forty minutes I was back in the same place. I took a right and as I swung around the bend we were confronted by a group of gendarmerie. Some were standing and some were kneeling, but all had their guns pointed at my head.

The next day, we made a management decision to split, and see if we could pick up some fare payers in the Milk Shop in Thessaloniki. About three hours out of Istanbul, there were several miles of roadworks, where the earth was excavated and piled on the banks, leaving a single track, in a kind of canyon. Half way along this, I saw a bus coming from the other direction, so I pulled up and got out of the bus, in order to discuss with the bus driver how to get past each other. As the bus got nearer he started to honk his horn repeatedly, and ever more frenetically, but he hardly slowed down. He just crashed headlong into us, for no apparent reason. Perhaps there were no functioning brakes on the vehicle.

There then followed a huge argument in which I grabbed the keys from the ignition to his bus, but after twenty minutes of this, I realised how pointless it was. His bus had no number plate and he had no licence. The best information I could get from him was that his name is Ali and he comes from Istanbul. We went to the nearest police station and gave them a statement, which took over two hours and seven coffees, before it finally dawned on me that it was a lost cause. The bus was still fine, just badly bent, so we carried on.

I don't know why but Sonia was nearing the end of her tether. Perhaps it was the poor food, guns in faces, driving many thousands of miles, having her clothes stolen while we were sleeping in the bus, or crashing into another bus. Or maybe it was something I said? I suggested she sleep in the back while I continue driving. I thought she was in bad need of a short surprise holiday. I crossed into Greece, while she was sleeping, and took the next turning left. I knew we would eventually reach the sea, and I hoped it would be in a nice spot with sandy beaches.

Just as the sun was setting, I drove down the mountains and landed on a wonderful yellow sandy beach, somewhere in the Strymonic Gulf. Sonia was still sleeping, so I woke her up. She said, "Where are we?" I said, "On a beautiful sandy beach in Greece. We are on holiday now." We found a lovely little cantina, overlooking the beach, and enjoyed a Greek salad and a bottle of Retsina wine, in this tranquil setting. Apart from the noisy ubiquitous cicadas of course.

Afterwards-as the beach was deserted, and it was such a pleasant warm evening- we decided to bed down on the beach, under the stars. We must have both been so tired, because we almost immediately fell to sleep. When we awoke the beach was no longer deserted. In fact there was a large circle of people around our sleeping bags watching our every move, which made it difficult to get up and get dressed. I assume this was not a tourist area, and they were unfamiliar with foreigners.

We spent a few days in the area and felt completely rested, ready to go on. We had discussed our next move and decided to go straight home from here, a drive of 1760 miles. The only stop we made was in Germany, at a large VW garage, to get the bus serviced. It had done a lot of work and was not driving well. When we arrived home, I had the repairs done to the damaged bodywork, caused by the crash in Turkey. When I got around to totting up the money we had made, after taking into account all the expenses, and the cost of the bodywork repairs, the profit came to a grand total of eight pounds. A good experience, a good laugh, but not a great financial success story. However, it did give me the idea to import Turkish sheepskin coats.

Flying Tesserae.

First I needed to get some capital together, so I went in search of a job, and quickly found one, working as a driver for Reading Museum and Art Gallery. My allocated vehicle was to be an ambulance that had been discarded by the Ambulance Service as being too old and unsafe. Sadly the blue light had been disconnected, and it had been sprayed a very unsafe dark maroon, but it had a good top speed and air suspension, which was great for driving off-road.

One of my first jobs was to go to the excavation site of two 4th century Roman buildings, overlaying a Roman pottery kiln, at Maidenhatch Farm, and recover the finds. A large amount of material was recovered from the site and added to the Museum's collection, mostly tiles, bones, and potsherds as well as bags of tesserae and mortar. It was located in the middle of the new M4 motorway construction site, somewhere near Pangbourne. The construction company had bowed to pressure, possibly from the Court, to allow the archaeologists as much time as possible to recover their finds. They had left an earth island, connected by a clay causeway, and excavated around it to a depth of perhaps twenty five feet. After heavy rainfall it had become unsafe, so the site had to be closed.

I was to drive over this causeway and load up the remaining finds and a few tools and the disassembled tin shed, before the final destruction of the site. I completed this task and parked up on the solid mainland to smoke a cigarette, while I surveyed the site. My last view was of a large excavator crossing the causeway and ripping up a mosaic floor, depicting a hunting scene, and watching the tesserae flying all over the place.

Another role I had was to move items back and forth from the Museum to their store on a nearby industrial estate. This unassuming store was a huge warehouse, with very few windows, containing wondrous treasures. Everything they could not display for political reasons, or did not want to display for reasons such as space constraint, was stored here. There was a dugout canoe, found in the Thames; a shrunken head; Chinese opium pipes; valuable works of art; and an Egyptian mummy, half unwrapped. One of the most surprising items was a Georgian Egyptian mummy grinding mill, used to grind mummies into a fine powder to be taken as an aphrodisiac.

My most important job was to drive all over the country to collect paintings by Sir Stanley Spencer, for an upcoming exhibition of his works. I would collect them from some surprising places, like the board room of a rather dirty engineering factory near Liverpool, or a private apartment in a mansion house in London, but most would come from other Museums and Art Galleries. Because of the high value of some of these paintings, the management would often insist I take a Museum gallery attendant with me. They would do exactly the same as they did in the Museum, just sit there, like statues and say nothing.

The most valuable painting came from the Manchester Museum and Art Gallery, and it was huge. In fact it was so big it protruded from the back of my van by about ten feet, so I tied a rag in the end of it, which is what I thought was the correct way to do it. I was just driving off when the Museum director came running after me, horrified I should even think of driving off like this, especially as it had just started raining.

The pay was not great, but I was able to supplement this by sleeping in the back of the van, and taking my own sandwiches, instead of spending my overnight allowance. I had the money set aside from the sale of my VW bus, so in time, I was able to save enough for my next project. Just as well really because I was sacked anyway. Apparently one of the Museum gallery attendants had caught me driving whilst eating my lunch and steering with my knee. I can see now why the Museum attendants are not often allowed out.

Sheepskins From Istanbul.

The plan was to buy a cheap car, drive it to Istanbul, and buy as many top quality Turkish sheepskin coats as my capital will allow. With the help of the Exchange & Mart I quickly found a suitable car, a 1958 Singer Gazelle for £65. I was banking on Singer's cars being as good as their sewing machines. I was planning to take about five days to drive there, five days to find and buy the merchandise and five days to drive home. Three weeks overall, what could go wrong?

Sonia had politely asked to be excused from this trip, since she had just started working for an insurance broker in Henley-on-Thames, although I suspected she was not ready for another trip. This would be the first time we had ever been apart. I invited my old mate Hugh and another friend, Steve. They both gladly accepted. We were going to leave around the end of October 1970, hopefully before the bad weather set in.

The drive through Central Europe went quite smoothly, although the weather had deteriorated considerably, and there was plenty of snow and ice on the roads. In Germany we picked up a hitch-hiker, a West Indian named George. He had worked in London sweeping the streets for seven years before deciding, on the spur of the moment, to make a break for it. He had no idea where he was going or how he would get there. We all got on so well and had a jolly drive.

By the time we got to Eastern Slovenia, we were ready for a night in a hotel, since we could not all sleep in the car. We quickly found one on top of an inactive volcano. It was a wonderful mediaeval castle, or at least a fortified house. Quite run down, extremely cheap and empty of guests it was a perfect match for our requirements. The only issue was that the owner only had double bedded rooms, so we took two anyway, and drew lots to see who slept with whom. The drop from our bedroom window was memorable. That evening we sat in the courtyard, drinking strong black coffee, watching the sun disappear behind the volcanic peaks in the distance. It was magical. George said, "I'm getting there."

We made an early start with Belgrade in our sights, a distance of just over 300 miles. Arriving there in mid-afternoon we managed to get hopelessly lost near the centre. We asked for directions from several people, and they cither didn't speak any English, or they were unfriendly. When we asked a policeman on point duty if he spoke English, he simply said, "Get out." Finally we saw three girls and stopped to ask them. One spoke passable English. She said, "Come to my friend's flat. We will have a small party and you will be able to sleep there."

We spent the evening with them talking, eating, drinking and smoking dope. I was surprised that there was so much dope smoking in Serbia. According to these girls they were all at it. All locally grown they said, and excellent quality, I must say. One of the girls took me to a pharmacy in the morning, to help me buy some medication for my chest. Even walking down the street, people were shouting insults at us, and it took three attempts to find a shop that would serve us. I have no idea what they objected to. What an unfriendly country this is.

We arrived safely in Istanbul and installed ourselves in a cheap hotel, near the Pudding Shop, which was becoming quite famous. George stayed with us for a couple more days before going his own way, heading East. I hope he found what he was looking for, he was such a kind intelligent man. I set to work straight away, looking for the kind of merchandise I had seen on a previous trip. My starting point was the leather working area of the Grand Bazaar.

After several trips, some red herrings and an attempted elaborate rip-off, I found exactly what I had been seeking. Fourteen superb hand-embroidered ladies sheepskin coats, better than any I had ever seen before. The dealer knew he had a desirable and superior product, so my attempts at negotiating the price were hard work, and didn't get me much of a price reduction. The deal was done, we were loaded and on our way back home. Good, I was really missing Sonia.

This was the start of my problems. We crossed into Bulgaria with no issues, other than a thorough search by the Bulgarian customs officials. Heavy snow was starting to fall on already icy cobblestone roads that had poor traction at the best of times. After only twenty miles the road was blocked by a massive truck pulling a similar size trailer. His mate was reversing up in a similar size gig, to try and pull him out, using a long steel cable. Something just didn't look right to me, something to do with the weight of the loads, or the size or length of the cable made it look unsafe. I shouted to the others to stand well back, and as the truck took the strain, the cable exploded into its component parts. The hurling end broke the sound barrier causing a loud crack. Anyone standing within range would have been beheaded for sure.

When we reached the Yugoslavian border, they would not let us in with these goods. They refused point-blank, telling me that my merchandise must be in a sealed container with the correct paperwork. The only option seemed to be to find some sacks in which to load the coats, stitch them up and send them by train to the Austrian border, using a shipping agent. This was going to have a serious impact on my profit margin, but I could see no alternative. The custom guard said he had a friend that could supply the sacks. I agreed that he should phone him. When this horrible, greasy, aggressive, fat (you can see I am not liking him already) man appeared, he wanted the same for six rotten potato sacks as I had paid for my car, but I had no choice.

When we got to the goods sidings, this side of the border, I had to pay even more for a shipping agent to complete some pointless, simple forms, and the cost of the shipping. At this point Steve, who had done no travelling like this before, could stand no more. He bailed out and took the train all the way home. We continued battling through the snow and ice to arrive at the other end of Yugoslavia, just on the Slovenian/Austrian border, to retrieve my shipment. Unfortunately the same situation applied in Austria. I had no alternative other than appointing another shipping agent, this time shipping them back to England.

Nothing left to do but drive home in this appalling weather. On the outside I looked fine, but inside I was screaming, "I'm cold, I'm hungry, I miss my wife, I miss my home, I want this to end." Hugh seemed completely unperturbed by all this. Shortly after entering Austria we came to a long hill that I simply could not summit because of the snow. After several attempts I reversed a long way back to a snow free tunnel and put my foot down, to gain as much speed as possible. We just managed to make the summit, but it was so scary, knowing for certain that death played along the curb.

Coming down the other side, the car in front had to stop, and I just could not, and drifted, at slow speed, into his boot. He was so kind and friendly, and understood I had no chance of stopping without chains, which were obligatory in winter, in most of central Europe. Considering I had bashed up the back of his car, he could not have been nicer.

We were now on the German Autobahn system, which had been cleared of snow with snow ploughs, and gritted to melt the ice. A lovely chance to put my foot down and kill some miles. Hurtling through the night, at top speed, there was a sudden grinding noise, followed by a bang, at which point the back wheels left the road, in a kind of pole volt motion. A large steel rod smashed its way through the floor of the car, narrowly missing Hugh. What had happened was that the drive shaft had failed, the front end had dropped down, embedding itself into the tarmac, leaving engine debris strewn along the Autobahn.

Within minutes two traffic cops in brown leather jackets arrived. They were really friendly, believe me they are not always, and they said they would tow us to a nearby garage. We sat with them in their warm car as they fixed a tow-rod. One of the back wheels had seized. As we bumped and rattled along they were killing themselves with laughter. One of them said it was the funniest incident he had attended, since a van carrying sex-toys from Sweden crashed, spilling its load across the road, in what became known as the *Penis in Road* incident.

They dropped us outside a garage, in the middle of nowhere, and informed me the owner would be able to help me when the garage reopened, after the weekend. We wrapped ourselves in anything we could find to try and keep warm, but it didn't work. It was so cold, so much colder than it ever gets in England, I was probably near to hypothermia for the second time in my life. Feeling seriously in danger, we abandoned everything and took to walking, in the hope of meeting a vehicle.

I was beginning to lose my will to live, and sense of time, when a minibus pulled up. The driver was dressed in lederhosen, as often worn by Hitler Youth, when not on duty. He was playing yodel music on the radio. Yodelling is a kind of music that has a rapid change in pitch, from a low pitch chest sound, to a high pitch falsetto. It was said to have been devised so the Alpine cow-herders could communicate with their wives, in their village below the mountains, to tell them what time they would be back for dinner. This is the situation I find myself in, on Sunday 6th December 1970, and the last thing I can remember before reaching home.

Shirts from Marrakesh.

After I had a chance to recover from my journey, Sonia said, "Was it a success then?" I replied, "Yes, I learnt a lot." She said, "Like what?" I replied, "Well I learnt what a great weapon silence is, when deployed at the right time, while negotiating; I learnt to always have a budget before I go off buying stuff; oh yes, and never try to cross Europe in the middle of winter in an old banger." She said, "And did we make any money?" I replied, "Probably not much, but it depends on what I can sell them for."

As it happens I sold them effortlessly for a premium price. I did actually make a small profit, enough to finance my next enterprise. I knew what I was trying to achieve, which was simply to be able to earn a living working for myself, doing what I wanted, and travel while doing so. I thought, with what knowledge I had picked up, it should be possible to make a living importing a certain type of clothing, let's call it hippy clothing. Anyway I wouldn't be going far for the next few weeks, since we had to move home for the third time, and collect enough cash for another shipment.

We decided together, although Sonia may have said *I decided*, the next trip should be to Marrakech. Although I have been to Morocco before, I had never made it to Marrakech, and I really wanted to go there. I went for a more reliable vehicle this time, and found a 1952 VW Beetle for fifty pounds. Everything seemed to work on it, except the heater, which was permanently on, unless I got underneath and inserted a bolt, which would turn it permanently off.

I also had a plan, which was to buy as many Moroccan hand-woven cotton shirts as my funds would allow; use a shipping agent to get them back to England, and sell them by mail order and among friends. I had a budget too, which was to buy them for less than ten shillings, and sell them for more than thirty shillings, whilst spending as little as possible on the journey there and back. Looks like I am learning some stuff now. Sonia wanted to come on this trip.

We set off in March 1971, just as the weather was improving. The journey went reasonably well with only minor issues: The heater was permanently on, and we only had two cassette tapes for the whole journey: The Incredible String Band's album *Layers of the Onion,* which included *The Hedgehog Song,* and Bob Dylan's *Blond on Blond* album. Hours and hours driving along, listening to just these two tapes has a serious effect on my musical education.

When we entered the Saville area, in the autonomous region of Andalusia in Spain, we had to pass through a deserted customs post. Then we started to eat oranges. They were huge, juicy, delicious and cheap. Sonia peeled so many, her thumb became swollen and possibly infected. Oranges, *The Hedgehog Song, I Want You.* There was some relief when we left Seville and continued to Algeciras, for the ninety minute crossing to Ceuta, in Spanish Morocco. How could the Spanish maintain this stronghold and still whinge on about Gibraltar?

It was pleasant driving through Morocco with the warm days and cool evenings. The days were so warm, it was time for me to get under the car and fix the heater to permanently turn it off. Our Beetle was driving very well, although I had noticed there was some play on the steering, but nothing to be too concerned about. We decided to take a short break in Tetouan, and have a look around the Casbah in the Old City. The smells in the Casbah were something else. I could make out sandalwood, jasmine, mint tea, tobacco, keef , chicken scat, rosemary and orange juice mixed with the smell of donkey.

For no apparent reason, other than to get in the mood of this wonderful exotic country, we entered a shop selling antique guns. I started to negotiate for a pair of long flintlock guns called Moukahla. The ones I wanted were an Italian *roman lock* type and were about six foot long. The owner claimed they were made by a local factory around 1850 and were genuine, but I have no idea if this is true. Being the first customer of the day to enter his shop, I knew that the shopkeeper would regard it as auspicious to achieve a sale. I managed to get them for what I thought was a good price. I asked myself if it was a good price if I didn't need to buy two flintlock guns, or even have a place for them in the car.

We only drove 160 miles the next day, and made a further stop at Fes, before crossing the Atlas mountains. We spent two days wandering the old walled part, called *Fes el Bali,* and other parts of the Medina. The exotic aromas were all present but, noticeably, petrol fumes were not hanging in the air, as they often are. I mentioned this to our hotel manager and he said, "The Medina is the largest traffic free area in any city in the world." I can well believe it. It felt and looked very mediaeval. I knew it was recognized as the mercantile centre of Morocco. I considered doing my buying here, but decided to carry on the Marrakesh, and look there first.

We had a great time in Fes, wandering around the manufacturing area. I saw hundreds of small workshops comprising two or three people working gold, copper, cotton, wood and leather. There was also a huge dyeing area with numerous circular vats, covering all the primary colours, and of course, workshops making fez hats. The tanning area was an important industry for the city, but we didn't hang about for long in that area, due to the foul smell. It was the urine they used in the leather-tanning process, which was collected in piss pots from the neighbourhood, and had been for nearly a millennium, much as it used to happen in England in the Middle Ages.

It was a joy to sit outside one of the many tea houses, watching life happen, and trying to understand exactly what was going on. Every niche, large or small, commercial or social, seemed to be filled by someone. There were mad people, greedy people, rich, busy, lazy, poor, unhealthy and fit people represented, and mostly they seemed happy. I wondered what it was that held a nation back and stopped them developing. Perhaps they just didn't want to, or were not prepared to make the cultural sacrifice that seems to be implicit in development. Deep down I probably knew it was their religion. Anyway I just loved it as it is.

I was really looking forward to crossing the Atlas Mountains. There is something in certain names that I find gives the place an irresistible allure, and Atlas Mountains is one. Tizi n' Test is another, and the place we were aiming for. It was 440 miles from Fes, and since a lot of it would be mountain driving, the journey would probably take at least two days.

The Low Atlas were impressive, with the backdrop of snow capped peaks of the High Atlas, but the roads were not impressive. The play in the steering was deteriorating at the same pace as the roads. Now there was about two inches of play on the steering wheel. This is the land of the Berber people. We saw many examples of their villages hewn out of the rock. They were built in the mountains, of the mountains, and were therefore difficult to spot. We stopped at one busy market town that felt like it was a scene out of the Bible. There were stalls selling eye make-up made from various types of ground rock; fresh fruit and vegetables, some of which I had never seen before; goats heads; and the ubiquitous apothecary shop, with it's lines of jars containing some recognizable, and some unrecognisable animal body parts, plant roots, insects and minerals.

We had a delicious lunch comprising a vegetable tagine and flat bread, washed down with Coca-Cola and mint tea. This took place on a rooftop, looking out over the other rooftops, it became clear most social life happened on the rooftops. People were ordering stuff from the ground level and hauling it up in ropes, they were talking to other families and kids were flying kites. We couldn't stay long in this fascinating little place, because I wanted to make it to Tize n' Test before dark, so we could spend the night there.

Ascending the High Atlas, which separates the Mediterranean from the Sahara desert, was the most challenging drive of my life to date, made even worse by the dodgy steering. Making one last death defying turn Sonia said, "There it is. Welcome to Tizi n' Test Pass, 2052 metres. But where is the town? Where will we stay tonight?" I said, "Don't worry, there is a little wooden hut over there. We can ask." Inside the hut were two men sitting around a wood stove with a pot of mint tea boiling on top.

I said, "Good evening, would you please direct us to the town of Tizi n' Test." One of the men replied in broken English, "There is no town." Sonia said to me, "Buy a ******* map next time you want to cross a mountain range." I said, "Sorry. But look at that amazing starlit-sky." She said, "Just don't say another word." We spent a miserable, cold night sitting by the tiny wood stove. Tomorrow has to be a better day.

We set off at dawn for the last downhill eighty miles to Marrakech, travelling very slowly due to the worsening steering situation. It was so bad by now that I could only vaguely aim the car in the right direction, and slow right down or even stop if a car came the other way. I could think of no other alternative than to carry on. There was obviously nowhere to get the steering fixed before Marrakesh, and anyway it wasn't far now. Sonia said "How is the steering now?" I replied "A bit worse, but mostly much better."

We reached Marrakesh safely and checked into a hotel we had heard about. I was talking to some other travellers staying in the same hotel. I related the story of our adventures in the High Atlas, Tize n' Test, wood-stove, steering, the road from Fes. One of them said "Hang on a minute, you don't go through Tizi n' Test unless you are heading south, from Marrakech to Agadir." I went bright red, broke into a sweat. How could I find the words to tell Sonia? We would probably never see the Tize n' Test pass, not town but *pass*, again, so would I need to tell Sonia? When you love someone you just don't have secrets so I would tell her, just not yet. Hopefully I may forget in time.

My first priority was to get the car fixed, so I searched for a VW service centre. One did not exist but I was pointed in the direction of Mahmud, who apparently had the best VW *ear* in the city, and could diagnose any problem by listening to the car engine. Not sure how that would help with my steering problem, but I gave him a try. When he got underneath the vehicle, he immediately spotted the problem as being the failure of the link. When he showed me the failed part I again broke out into a sweat. It was a round piece of laminated rubber and leather with one large hole and two small holes in it. It had almost completely failed. Had this happened on the road it would have left me with no steering.

With this job out of the way and the car now safe to drive I could turn my mind to the main mission, which was to buy as many cotton unisex shirts as my budget would permit. We headed off to the market, passed the line of blind beggars, past the old slave-market to the workshop area. I started to talk to the owners and started to learn. One of the first things I learnt was if you were being hassled to buy, simply say *La shakrun,* and touch your heart with your right hand. This is the best way of saying, "Sincerely no thank you, and by the way, I am not a tourist and I have been to Morocco before." It is polite and friendly and seems to be recognized throughout north Africa.

I could not find what I wanted straight away, so I returned to the market several times and even started to get to know a few people. Initially the product was too expensive, not right or not available in sufficient quantities. After some perseverance I found an old man who seemed to have exactly what I was looking for. I brought Sonia back to seek her opinion. He offered me a diamond encrusted gold dagger for Sonia, I asked for two daggers, but he refused, so we got down to talking about shirts.

After protracted negotiations, lasting for four glasses of mint tea, we agreed on a quantity and price. I learnt the term Free on Board (F.O.B.) means I would pay the freight and customs clearance on arrival. The long sleeve shirts were made of hand loom cotton, brightly coloured with little diamond-shaped pieces of different coloured cotton sewn on. I placed my order for different colourways and sizes and I paid him in cash. I had travelled enough in the Arab world to know that this man would keep to his side of the bargain, so I trusted him.

Back at the hotel I met a middle-aged man called Keva and his young girlfriend. He said "When we are both back in England we should meet in London, where I live. I have had a great deal of success selling dolls mail-order by advertising in the News Of The World. I think we could do this with the shirts you have bought." I said, "Yes, I will definitely contact you and we can see if we can work anything out." He also told me that the sounds of Marrakesh, at dawn or dusk, were special, and that I should sit and listen to them.

That afternoon, just before dusk, I went for a mint tea by myself. As I settled down I started to listen. Bird songs; two women having a humdinger in the Old Slave Market; a man repeating his call to buy fresh orange juice, over and over again; urgent tapping of men working copper in the Jew's Market; donkey braying; some chickens; a man shouting *burro, burro,* which means heavily loaded donkey coming through; children playing; a sewing machine. Then it started, the *Adhan*, the strange musical wailing of the *Muadhin*, calling all believers to evening prayer. First one, with others following shortly afterwards, probably in some hierarchical order, spreading across the city in perfect harmony with the growing shadows of the setting sun.

We had completed the task so it was time to leave Marrakesh, which we did with some sadness and hope that we would return some day. We had agreed that we would try to avoid as many mountains as possible, by taking the coastal road. We headed for Essaouira. I had heard it was a great place to visit and not yet damaged by fans, following in the footsteps of Jimmy Hendrix, who had stayed a couple of years earlier, and is the place he is supposed to have written *Castles in the Sand*.

Arriving at Essaouira is a pleasant experience. Off white buildings with bright blue windows and doors, which I seem to remember as the colour that deters flies. The Atlantic coast was a mixture of rock and sand with deep blue ocean and thundering Atlantic rollers. It was a small city built in the eighteenth century, largely by the English architect Ahmet el

Inglizi. He famously abandoned Christianity for Islam and joined the *Salle Rovers*, a dreaded band of Barbary pirates, before taking up his position working for the Sultan of Morocco. He was helped by one Theodore Cornut, who did a nice job designing the Kasbah area.

Essaouira was a lovely place to spend a few days relaxing. We were sleeping on the beach at night, which meant we had to unload the car every night, since the door lock was broken. We piled our belongings in a heap at the end of our sleeping bags and stood the six foot long flintlock guns by our heads. This gave the appearance of some kind of Bedu camp of rebels which attracted the unwanted attention of the local police. It was no great problem though as the guns had blocked barrels.

We took our time working our way up the coast and enjoying every bit of it. The only exception was Casablanca which neither of us liked. It is the largest city in Morocco and the industrial centre of the country. It was full of ugly, half built concrete industrial buildings, monstrous blocks of flats, dirty shopping areas and polluted rammed-roads. It is as though they had abandoned all sense of charm and beauty for the pursuit of modernism and money in a desperate attempt to become a modern European-style city. It didn't work for us and probably not for them either.

The remainder of the journey home was pretty uneventful. Hours of driving to the tunes of Bob Dylan and The Incredible String Band. Just the two of us and our two guns. We arrived home in April and moved straight into our new home back in Henley-on-Thames. We were sharing a small cottage with friends in New Street, which of course is the oldest street in town. It is a lovely little cottage with a pretty walled garden, that was once inhabited by Prince Russell's favourite whore, or so it was said,

Reading Rock Festival.

Soon after we had settled into our new home, I received notification that my consignment had arrived. It was the correct weight and the correct number of sacks, so it proved that I had been right to trust that old trader in the Kasbah in Marrakech. I immediately set about finding a clearing agent, so I could get the goods as soon as possible, and crack on selling them. The agent quickly telephoned me back to say that he needed a hand loom licence, to effect clearance, and that I needed to apply for one quickly in order to mitigate storage-charges.

I worked my way through several government departments but, days later, I had still made no progress. I decided to drive to London and visit the issuing government department in person. I arrived around ten and asked the lady on the reception where I could get this paperwork. She said she would let someone know I was waiting.

I sat waiting for hours, while asking the receptionist at regular intervals. At one on the dot, everyone in the office left for lunch, leaving me alone with my thoughts. Soon after two they all returned, including a Scottish man who said, "Are you still waiting young man? You had better come upstairs to my office." We sat down at this huge desk underneath a portrait of the Queen, and he introduced himself as the Department Head. He said "We make it as difficult as possible for casual importers to obtain a licence. I admire your perseverance. Here is your hand loom licence. Safe journey home young man."

I was able to collect the consignment, take them back to our little cottage, rip the bails open and inspect the goods. They were exactly as I had ordered, I just needed to sell them. I thought I needed a trading name, so, for the princely sum of one pound, I registered the rather grand sounding name of *The Mediterranean Trading Company,* and obtained my free listing in the Thompson Yellow Pages. Within days I started receiving calls. "Please can I have a quotation for the shipment of 27 million tons of coal from Poland to Iran; I would like to buy 300 KG of best *Kalamata* olives; I would like to work my passage to Scilly, do you have a ship going that way with a space on board?"

I decided to take up Keva's offer to discuss selling my products via mail order, so I took a trip up to London to see him at his flat. We agreed on an advertising plan, prices and his cut. He then rolled a spliff to cement the deal. I became so stoned I could hardly move. I had never taken anything as strong as this. He was just a little stoned and he started telling me his life story. Of Hungarian Jewish extraction, he had escaped the Nazis, and arrived in London before the war started. He had spent much of his time hanging out with fellow Jew Ronnie Scott, at his club, selling cannabis to his mates and smoking some along the way.

I was surprised when he described how ubiquitous cannabis was, during and just after the war, especially among the jazz lovers and the bohemian class. He told me he used to meet Burmese sailors at the docks, and buy pillow cases full of the finest grass, for very little money. Although in the strict sense it was illegal, it was not of any great interest to law enforcers and not known about by the general public, so it was smoked quite openly. A memorable evening, but I needed to crack on and sell these shirts, if I was ever to make a living from trading.

I had heard that the *Windsor Jazz Festival* was about to morph into the first ever *Reading Rock and Pop Festival,* and that tents were available for the selling of merchandise. I booked a tent using the money from the first few sales of shirts I had made to friends. It was reasonably priced and came with the advantage of three car parking spaces and twelve tickets. Which was great because I was able to immediately recover my investment by selling two car parking spaces and six entry tickets, for the going rate of £2. The tent was located really close to the stage, so the view of the performing bands was fantastic.

We saw just about all the performances by all the bands, which included *East of Eden, Wishbone Ash, Ralph McTell, Genesis, Rory Gallagher* and *Osibisa.* For me, the musical highlight was a local lad called, *The Crazy World of Arthur Brown,* performing *Fire!,* which was outstanding. The US President Richard Nixon had just declared his *war on drugs,* a few days before the start of the festival. The newly formed Reading Drugs Squad became rather over-excited by these vegetable-wars, and busted over one hundred people, including a French diplomat, a Red Cross first-aider and a vicar.

We had a great festival and I sold lots of shirts but I didn't get a good price for them. The quality was poor, and after the first wash, they shrank by about a third and the colours ran. Fortunately a lot of the people buying them didn't wash their clothes often, if at all. Another lesson I had learnt the hard way. I made a decision that I would only ever buy or deal in quality, whatever the product.

Throughout the festival various people brought a variety of goods for me to sell. They were made in cottages, farms and communes from across the country. I made far more money selling these things than I did selling my Moroccan shirts. I paid a visit to Keva in London to sort out the precious few sales and tot up the cash. On the return journey my old VW Beetle gave up the ghost, so I gave it to a friend who subsequently recovered it and swapped it for a mandolin. A fitting tribute to the old girl, I thought, and probably the end of another chapter.

Ireland, Safe From The Atom Bomb

We were still living in Henley-on-Thames, and we had friends there, but we had maintained contact with our friends in Reading. Some of these friends were at, or had dropped out of Reading University. It was around the peak of the *Cold War,* and there was a genuine fear of an imminent atomic bomb attack. Jack and Maureen had bought a place on the West Coast of Ireland, near Sligo, and had moved their life there. Shortly after, Leaf bought a house nearby, followed by two more friends. Apparently, it was about as far west as it was possible to go in Europe, and having no nearby strategic targets, was unlikely to be at the receiving end of a Russian Atomic bomb. I heard it was very beautiful and peaceful with an abundance of cheap houses.

We decided to join our friends and also look for a place. Apparently most of the properties were semi-derelict and unwanted by the locals, who preferred to live in modern boxes with running water and electricity. All our friends had paid exactly £2000 for their houses, so I assumed that was the going rate. I did not have the cash so I approached my Grandma, who was happy to lend it to me.

We set off to Eire by car in late summer. I was surprised at the distance and the difficulty of the journey, involving a long ferry crossing and a difficult drive diagonally across the country on poor roads, but I suppose that is the whole point. Two days later we were comfortably ensconced with our friends and ready to go looking for a property.

Local intelligence had informed us that we should head to an estate agent called Kelly's, and meet Francis Kelly. Francis had a local reputation of being the *live wire* of the property world in the Sligo area. We met him, and he immediately started driving us around the countryside looking at property. He said, "Would you like to see a *tached* cottage?" I said, "Do you mean attached?" He said, "No, *tached*." I said, "Do you mean detached?" He said, "I will show you." When we arrived at the *thatched* cottage the owner was on the roof, with a pitch fork. He was apparently *re-thatching,* although it looked more like he was building a hay stack.

We carried on visiting properties, as Francis tried to turn every negative aspect into a positive one. Viewing the cottage with the six inch square kitchen window, Francis said, "It won't cost you much to paint that." The cottage with the crack down the length of the wall, he said, "It's nice to get some air and sunlight in the place." Eventually we found a small, three room, rather ugly grey concrete-cottage in beautiful surroundings. It came with an acre of orchard and an acre of pasture and a large barn. The house was located on top of a small hill and the view over the tiny fields, with the stuks of corn, to the distant hills was breathtaking. I said, "How much?" He said, "Just a couple of thousand." I said, "Two thousand?" He said, "No a couple, but I might be able to get it down to two and a half." We finally settled on £2000.

We needed to find a solicitor to sort out the sale. We were advised by Leaf to go to a Mr. Charley Brown of Argue and Phibbs, in Sligo. I would find out if I could trust a solicitor with such an unbelievable name. I found their office in the town, and was delighted at how easy this one time Crown solicitor was to deal with. I made an appointment to meet the property owner in Charlie's office the next day, who turned up, covered in cow shit. We seamlessly completed the paperwork, I handed over the cash and it belonged to us. We were now the proud owners of a grubby, derelict cottage with an orchard full of dead apple trees and a collapsing barn.

We had a few days left in Ireland so we set to work cleaning, painting and generally making the place look lived in. We even had friends over for dinner, and sat around the fire, watching it convert vast amounts of the wood I have chopped from the dead apple trees into heat, which disappeared up the straight chimney. I bought some saplings and carefully planted them along our border, in the hope that there would be a vibrant hedge when we next returned. When we eventually left for home, I took one last look over my shoulder at our little house, only to see a cow pulling up and munching on the trees I had just planted.

Life on the Thames.

We had moved from the cottage in New Street to another shared cottage, in a Thames side hamlet, just outside Henley, called Mill End. There was a small community of nine other dwellings. It was a very friendly place to live, and we had a lot of fun living there. It was a lovely place to spend warm Sunday afternoons. Picnics soon became quite a regular feature.

One weekday evening, after dark, there was a knock at the door. A young man was standing there, dripping wet, looking traumatised. He said, "Me and my mate were fishing in a punt, by the weir, when it turned over. Now I can't find my mate." Sonia sat him down, gave him a cup of sweet tea and phoned the Fire and Rescue Service. Meanwhile I carried my canoe to the water's edge and launched it in the direction of the weir. I paddled up and down the river for over an hour, until I caught sight of the up-turned punt floating past. It was the creepiest thing I have ever seen, and it haunted me for some time afterwards. Of course there was no sign of the other fisherman.

Back at the house, I took the phone call from his young wife; that haunted me for some time as well. I had to explain how her husband and father of her young child had been taken away from her. What started out as such a fun, healthy thing to do, should end in death was such a tragedy. It would take me a long time to get over the sound of her disbelief followed by her wails of grief. I decided, there and then, if I ever had children they would learn to swim.

I was fed up sharing my home with other people, so we decided to rent somewhere on our own. The picture framing was going through a bit of a resurgence, with much of the work coming through my Mother's little art shop in Henley. My father-in-law, Stanislav, had offered us a workshop in the old stable block, at their home in Reading, so it made sense to look for a house there.

This proved much more difficult than I thought it would. After looking at numerous houses and failing to rent them, I eventually found a house opposite the abattoirs, in Great Knollys Street. It was a small Victorian two bedroom terrace house that the West Indian owner was planning to convert into two flats. In reality it was a slum, being very damp and covered in mould, but at least we did not have to share it, for now.

The landlord made a poor attempt to convert it into two flats. The downstairs bathroom was to be shared. The hot water system consisted of a Baby Burco electric tea-earn, balanced on two planks, on the end of the bath, and was potentially lethal. Things really deteriorated when the landlord let the top floor to another couple. It got so bad that one evening the upstairs tenant, angered by us allegedly using his toilet roll, kicked our door down, resulting in us calling the police. We had to move out immediately to a room offered to us by Sonia's parents.

Poland.

It was a culturally interesting experience, living with the Papierowski family. One day, when I was helping Stanislav lay a concrete path in their garden, I asked him about his life in Poland. This is what he told me:

"I was born in the mediaeval city of Poznan, on the River Warta, one of the oldest cities in Poland. I was born German since Poznan was part of the German Empire, but that changed after the Great War, when it again became part of a reborn Poland. When I finally left Poland for the last time, it was again occupied, this time by Nazi Germany.

I was always good at making things, so my father got me a job as an apprentice for a local well known factory, making high quality cabinets for gramophones, amongst other things. My first job was to make all my tools. I made planes, rebate planes, spokeshaves, mallets, clamps, mitre blocks and many other tools. It was a good apprenticeship and it worked out well for me. I learnt many things about building furniture, and also how to finish the pieces. I learnt how to mix and apply my own French polish, and how to make my own glue by boiling bones. As part of my final exams I had to design and make my own item. I chose to make a wooden box, using steam to make the round case, and decorated it with different types of inlaid-wood, in the shape of an asymmetric star. I passed all my exams and became fully qualified.

Since my company was exporting many designs of cabinets to England, they thought it would be a good idea to send me there to visit some customers, and discuss new designs. First I had to learn to speak at least *some* English, which I found very hard to learn. The visit worked out very well, because I was talking to other craftsmen so we could communicate in a technical language.

When I was not working I would spend my time walking in the forest; swimming in the river, even in winter; and practising on the parallel bars. Sometimes I would go to a dance with my friends from work. At one such dance I saw this beautiful young woman arrive. Straight away I said to my friend, 'That woman will be my wife.' I asked her to dance and she said yes. Her name was Anettka, She came from a small town just outside of the city. We fell in love and soon we became married. After only a short time we had a son, followed by another son.

Life was good in Poland. Our sons were growing up strong and healthy and doing well at school, and my job was going well. This all changed on 1 September 1939. I was at work as normal when I received a telegram from the Polish Air Force to immediately report to the Poznan-Krzesiny Air base. I was not permitted to go home first but to report for service immediately. I cycled to the base, and on the way there, I saw many Nazi planes fly over. When I arrived near the base, I stood on top of a hill and looked down on a scene of utter devastation. Most of the planes were laying around the runway, in flames.

I was instructed to rejoin my reserve unit at a nearby base, so I had to leave my City and my Family and make my own way to the other Airbase. By the time I arrived at my new base that also was in flames and I was informed that the Nazi tanks were on the move. Within nine days the Nazis had destroyed 90% of

Poznan. I did not know if my family was alive or not. I had no choice but to make my way to the Romanian border and try to join the exiled Polish Air Force there.

The journey on foot through Poland was difficult. I had to look out for Nazis all the time, they were everywhere. Ukraine was already full of Russian soldiers, so that was hard as well. Many weeks later, I crossed the border into Romania, but things were no better there. The *Iron Guard* was in power and they were cooperating with Nazi Germany, so I knew I would be handed over if I was caught by the Romanian Police. For this reason I avoided the large towns and just travelled by myself on foot. The local peasants in the country would often help me, passing me food and letting me sleep in their barns. Still the journey was difficult, especially crossing the swamps. I had to make this journey in the dead of winter.

I had many adventures along the way, most of which were bad, but there were always kind people to help me on my way. On one occasion I was wading through a fast flowing river, when I saw a girl taking her cow down to the water's edge to drink. Suddenly the cow ran into the river, and the rope became entwined around the girl's legs and dragged her in too. I could see she was drowning so I dove in, swam to her and pulled her to safety. I have often wondered what happened to that little girl.

My journey continued, through Bulgaria and right down to the bottom of Greece, until I finally reached the port of Piraeus, many months after leaving Poland. Here I was able to make contact with the Allied Forces and report for duty. I was fed, clothed and I could sleep in a safe, warm place. It was here that I received the first word from my family. In the Red Cross tent there was a notice-board, and unbelievably, there was a message from Anettka. It just said that she was well, and the boys were well, but that life was horrible under the Nazis.

I found out later how bad it was. My sons had to go to a Nazi school, where they were often beaten badly if they were caught speaking Polish. My oldest son had a really bad time when he was beaten on the head so badly, it probably affected him for the rest of his life. In Poznan at this time one could be shot for the smallest reason. Anettka's brother was dragged into the City Square and shot, because he had a flour grinding-stone hidden in his house. Under Nazi rule, most of the food production had to be sent to Germany, for the war effort. It was a death sentence if your grinding-stones, used to grind the flour to make bread, were not handed in to the Nazis. Her job was as part of a burial party, to bury the dead that had been executed or just died of starvation. This did mean she could have some food but how that affected her I will never know.

Finally I had rejoined the Polish contingent of the RAF. They wanted me because I spoke some English. I did not speak English well, but they were desperate to find a way of communicating with the Polish air crew. These Polish airmen had bravely fought on, for nine days after the b*litz-creed,* and the RAF wanted their skills and bravery on-board. I was sent to different RAF bases in Southern England, where I got on quite well.

Apart from my job, I was able to use my skills, to make a little money, and become useful to the English. I fixed the clock in the officer's mess, which had been broken for years. I made a canoe for my commanding officer, which was a great success, and he paid me well for it. In time, I was transferred to Arborfield Garrison, near Reading, where I was to join the Polish land forces in preparation for the D-Day landings.

After the main landings had taken place, and the beaches had been secured, we left in a large convoy. Our first stop was Holland. Here the people were in a sad state, Germany having cruelly cut off all supplies to Holland, in retaliation for the train drivers strike. Food was now coming into the country but the population, always clean by nature, were desperate for soap. I found I could make good money by dealing in soap on the black market. I knew I needed to make money, if I were ever to get my family back.

The convoy pressed forward relentlessly, and I saw many horrible things on the way. I saw two English soldiers about to light a fire by throwing petrol onto a small flame. I shouted out to them to stop, but it was too late. The flame flashed back up the flow of petrol and exploded, killing them both. On another occasion there was an exhausted old woman laying in the road. My commanding officer ordered me to drive over her to avoid halting the huge column of lorries, but I would not. I made the driver stop the vehicle and I dragged the woman to the side of the road before continuing. My commanding officer threatened me with a court-martial, but nothing ever came of it.

After the war had been won, and I was safely back in England, my mind turned to my family, and how I could get them over here. Poland was now behind the Iron Curtain, and under the control of the Soviet Union, so returning home to Poland was not an attractive option. I had some money set aside now, and I did any work I could find to get enough to bring my family to England. When I had enough money I used my network of Polish and English friends to find a people-smuggler that could bring them to me.

The day came for them to leave. They were placed in three wooden-crates, containing large engineering machine-parts, packed in straw and loaded on the back of a large lorry, destined for the British-controlled zone of Berlin. The boys were told to keep quiet for the whole journey, as they set off on this frightening and arduous voyage into the unknown. Upon entry to the British Zone at a place called *Checkpoint Charlie,* the vehicle was thoroughly searched by the Soviet border guards, at one point pushing their bayonets into the packing cases, but all went well, for once.

Once in Berlin, they were able to travel by returning army lorries, as far as a port town in Northern France. From here they sailed on a fishing vessel landing on the beach in Brighton, sometime in 1946. They had nothing with them, other than the clothes they were wearing, and their knives and forks. My third son was born the next year, and four years after they arrived on the beach in Brighton, Sonia was born, as a refugee, in a camp in Checkendon, near Reading."

I said, "That was interesting. I'm ready for a cup of tea now." But I thought, "according to the Quran, *To save one life is like saving all mankind.* This man saved two!"

I have often thought about the knife and fork, and asked myself what items I would have brought with me. Anything of value would have long gone in Poland, and food would have been consumed during the journey. Photographs would have been rare at that time, and probably would not have survived the journey anyway, so perhaps a knife and fork is not such a bad idea. I wonder if they still exist?

Doctor Ali's Afghan Sheepskin Coats.

Although the picture framing business has ended, I was now achieving my first goal, which was to be able to support us both, by running our own business and still travelling. I had some capital, and I thought there must be good products, other than hand loom cotton, I could import from Morocco and sell to the growing number of *Head Shops* for the new so-called *Hippy* market. There were already products on the market like Afghan coats, Turkish blouses, Moroccan leather goods and *Goulimine* beads. I decided to send my friend, Matthew, off to Morocco, at my expense, to seek out new and viable products. This was a complete failure because I was unable to give him any sensible brief. It cost me a bit of money, but there were no bones broken or friendships damaged.

Along the way I had met various people, and one day a Scotsman named Charlie phoned me, out of the blue. He was working for a customs-clearing agent and I had first met him when importing my Turkish sheepskins. He said, "I have met an Afghan doctor who has a lot of Afghan sheepskin coats for sale. He fled Afghanistan, with his family, and he converted all his capital into Afghan coats. Would you like me to arrange a meeting?" I said, "Yes please."

I travelled to London and met Doctor Ali. in his horrible one room bedsitter he was sharing with his wife and children, while he awaited the outcome of his asylum hearing. It seemed sad that this softly-spoken, cultured, medical doctor should have been hammered down into the ground, through no fault of his own. He showed me some samples of his product and it looked good. He knew no one in England, and by his own admission, had no knowledge of business. He needed to sell and so he offered me a really good price, which I did not negotiate strongly. We had a deal.

I bought the first batch for cash, and loaded them into my new car. There followed many trips, back and forth from Henley-on-Thames to London, as I bought and sold these coats. I was selling in obvious places like Kensington Market, a three storey indoor market that was really the heart of the *Hippy* culture. Before the band Queen was formed, Roger Taylor ran a stall here, assisted by his employee Freddie Mercury. Lemmy, a leading member of Motorhead, sold his dope from here. It was a great place to sell, meet people, and buy new products, since many of the stallholders also wholesaled their products.

The business started to take off, with the Afghan coat sales being the core product. Ali was delighted and further developed his business, using his contacts back home to import more coats. I saw potential, so I asked my brother John if he would like to leave his secure and lucrative job, working for a pharmaceutical company, and join me. He had been selling an early version of the birth pill to doctor's practices. One evening with friends, through a cloud of smoke, we calculated he had single handedly reduced the national birth rate by 630,000 souls. Not bad for a year's work. John would be able to add a level of professionalism to the sales that would enhance the business.

Not long after John joined the business, Ali telephoned me. He said, "I am so pleased and excited to be able to tell you that I have been granted asylum. Since I will now be able to work as a doctor, I will no longer have the need to import Afghan sheepskin coats. I want to thank you, from the bottom of my heart, for the help you have given me, in starting my new life." That was a very nice thing to hear, but it wasn't really justified. I had bought something at a price and sold it for more. Well, I suppose I could have hammered him down on price more, but I still suffered from an outbreak of *Imposter Syndrome.*

Shortly after this phone conversation, Sonia, who had been handling these coats, broke out in a horrible rash. I then started hearing similar things from some of my customers. We decided it was some kind of dermatitis, so I sent the remaining stock to be professionally cleaned and treated, at great expense to myself. Still, I could continue the business using my new network of contacts, to buy different clothing and also, bags, joss-sticks, Indian jewellery, essential oils and the evocative *Goulimine* beads.

A Home At Last.

We decided it was time to revisit our little house in Sligo. This time, I would drive my transit van, which would enable us to take a lot more stuff and two friends, Andy and Caroline, who were also looking to buy a place in Eire. We had been offered Jack's house, since he was going to be away, and needed someone to look after it and his demanding cat we called Hitler. It was just as well we would be staying at Jack's, because when we went to our place, we found the cows had broken the front door down and filled every room with dung. It really was going to be a case of mucking out our house.

After our long journey I decided to have a bath, but of course nothing is simple at Jack's. He had built an enormous fibreglass bath that took up about a third of the footprint of the whole house. In order to fill the bath with an acceptable amount of hot-water, it was necessary to think forward. First I had to fire up my chain saw and cut a substantial amount of wood before firing up the boiler. It would then take several hours of intense heat, lots of banging and gurgling sounds to arrive at about two inches of water in the bottom of this huge bath. Hardly worth it.

The next day the four of us went for a walk that took us to the jaw-droppingly beautiful banks of Loch Gill. Right on the edge of the Loch was an unusually pretty stone built, thatched cottage and barn that appeared to be empty. Caroline said, "That is the cottage for us." I said, "Let us see if we can find the owner." We walked about half a mile up the track to the next house and knocked on the door. Andy said, "Is that your cottage?" He replied, "Yes. Would you be after buying it?" Andy said, "How much?" He replied, "I was thinking of around two thousand." Andy said, "I'll buy it."

And the deal was done. It was that simple. It only remained to mark out the size of the plot of land. The owner, Patrick, was the local police man, known as a Guarda. We took four poles, one each and set about marking the plot. There was a certain amount of, "To me; a little bit further that way; not that far;" before we arrived at the boundary lines. In all it was about an acre of fairly useless, damp-land, but what a wonderful property. They had a dream. To convert the barn into a pottery studio and sell their wares and cream teas to the steamer full of American tourists that arrived every morning, around eleven.

Deal agreed, we were all off to Patrick's local, which he referred to as his *office*, for a few jars. He explained that, on the rare occasion that a crime was perpetrated on his patch, he would go to his *office* and simply wait. Like the radio that was stolen from the Farley's house last week; within about two pints someone came up to him and said, "I see Jimmy has got a nice new radio."

After a few days of mucking out, repairing the front door and generally cleaning up our house, we were able to move back in. The first morning I went off to buy some supplies from old Mrs O'Sullivan's shop, which was really just a tin shed. I said, "Have you always had this shop?" She said, "Good Lord no. I married a rebel, and signed up to an Irish Republican Army unit, so I could kill the British. I could disassemble a Thompson gun, clean it, put it back together and have it firing again within six minutes. I was pretty good at shooting it too. But that was a long, long time ago." Nice to meet the neighbours I thought.

The journey home from Ireland was surprisingly long and arduous. By the time we reached Reading we had a new plan for our future, that involved buying a house in Reading. It made sense to let go of our little cottage in Ireland, so I could repay the loan to my Grandma, and put any profit towards a house in Reading. Fortunately I was able to sell the cottage to a friend almost immediately, and at a small profit. With that out of the way I was able to fully concentrate on finding a house and finding the money to buy it.

We did find a suitable house quickly. It was a semi-detached house on a 1930's housing estate, in a suburb of Reading. I was then confronted with the task of finding a Building Society that would lend me the money. This was going to be difficult, since they were demanding three years audited-figures for self-employed people, or a full-time job. I spoke to my friend Mike in London, who was in a similar position being in business himself. We both applied some creative thinking and developed our own kind of self-certified mortgage. He gave me a full time job; I applied and got a mortgage; he fired me. I then did exactly the same for him. The mortgage went through successfully, the deal was done and we had our own home.

On the day of completion we excitedly went to our new home, with a car full of the essential items to start living there. I found the correct street but I couldn't see the house. I said, "What number is it?" I realised I had forgotten to bring the address. All the houses looked identical, so I had to just guess. Feeling quite sure I had the right house I tried the key, but it didn't fit. A nervous looking woman opened the door. After I had explained my situation she said, "Try number 97." That wasn't it either, but I did find it eventually.

The Family Dog Shop.

I was doing my usual rounds of London, touting my sheepskin coats along Portobello Road, when I saw something strange. It was a large model nose, measuring about four by six feet, fixed to the front of a psychedelic painted building above a shop window. Immediately I identified this shop as being a potential customer, so I investigated it further. Looking through the window I could see the merchandise on display, which included bongs, chillums, hookahs, pipes, ponchos, Indian-shirts, Kashmir-blankets, Stars & Stripes joint-rolling papers, Afghan sheepskin coats, Kuchi dresses and, of course, Goulimine beads.

I went inside and asked, "Who is the buyer?" The assistant said, "You need to see Russell. You'll find him in his office on the next floor." I went upstairs and met Russell. He was tall, handsome, well dressed and spoke with a public school accent. I said, "I wondered if you would like to buy some of my Afghan coats?" He replied, "I buy nothing from Afghanistan unless it has a Government Gold Seal." From then on, we got on really well, and talked for ages over an espresso coffee and joint.

I asked, "What goes on in this amazing looking building?" He said, "Well the top floor I sublet to a publisher, responsible for publishing The Whole Earth Catalogue, The Last Whole Earth Catalogue, and Definitely The Last Whole Earth Catalogue Ever." This is an American counter-culture publication for people wanting to live a self-sufficient life, and for people interested in holism and ecology. It listed a wide range of tools, seeds, clothing, machines etc.. Its slogan is *Access to Tools*. The cover featured a picture of Planet Earth, after a long running public campaign for NASA to release the first ever photograph taken of Earth from Space.

Russell said, "Have you heard of Frendz?" I said, "No I haven't." He said, "Well it's an underground magazine, closely connected to *London Oz* and *Time Out*. That is published upstairs as well. On this floor I manufacture my *Stars & Stripes* and *Esmeralda Papers*. I get the papers manufactured and printed in Spain. It arrives in a huge roll, then I use this machine to cut and fold and package them. I am also trying to start a waterbed business, but I'm having difficulty finding a manufacturer for the frames and headboards. Would you be interested in getting involved?" I said, "Yes, I think I would, although I don't have any furniture building experience."

Russell continues, "Downstairs we have the shop. It was actually the first *Head Shop* in England, but one or two others have since opened up." I said, "This is all looking a bit Californian, what's the connection?" He said, "Actually I have dual-nationality and my father lives in the US, so I often go there. Waterbeds are big business over there." I said, "Let me have a think about what we can offer each other, and I'll come back and see you again soon. Meantime, I know you said you didn't have the cash to buy any sheepskin coats, but you may as well take some anyway, and see if you can sell them."

Driving home that evening, I started to think how I could make it work. I really liked Russell, he seemed so affable and open. Waterbeds were unheard of in England, but lots of new things were happening here, so it could well work. I could take a more sensible approach like Mike, who has just refused the exclusive on a sort of board thing on a roller-skate, that is also supposed to be big in the US. By the time I reached home I had already made up my mind. My existing business of wholesaling clothing-merchandise, could be left in the capable hands of John, for the sales and buying; and Sonia for all the administration and finances. I would offer Russell the manufacturing side for a 50% stake in his waterbed business.

Later that week, I made a return trip to The Family Dog Shop, and put my offer to Russell. He said, "You're on, partner." and we shook hands. I now had to find suitable manufacturing premises, people with the right skills, tools and equipment, a van, of course money to pay for it all, and a name. A trawl of the Reading area came up with a vacant print works, wedged between a bakery and a row of terraced houses. A visit to Barclays International Bank came up with the money to secure the lease on the premises, and the purchase of the machinery and van. Russell already had a concession in a large premises in the Kings Road; and a small shop in Portobello Road, not far from The Family Dog Shop. Aquarius Waterbeds sounded like a good name, so now I just had to find people with the skills to build the bed frames and headboards.

I bought a van, and decided it was necessary to have an elaborate paint-job done on it. It took a while to find a signwriter in Henley or Reading, that may be capable. I showed my new-found signwriter the design and asked, "Would you be able to paint this?" He said, "I was held in Colditz during the war. One of my jobs was to forge the *Urlaubsfchein* pass and other documents for Lieutenant Commander William Stephens. It was a leave pass in the name of Jean Barder, a French electrician employed by the Germans. The day Billy and Ronnie were going to escape Douglas Bader, who had eyes on the guards, was conducting the orchestra. Every time the guards looked away, they paused the music. Billy and Ronnie went through the kitchen window; took their civilian clothes off to squeeze through a narrow flue, on to the roof and away. It was a home run, that one was. So yes, I can do your paint-job.

now had everything in place. A friend with some minor DIY skills would be building the bed frames and a farmer in Cornwall had converted his barn to be able to do the radio welding of the plastic mattresses and safety liners. Actually the designs were quite simple, but measurement was the problem. Nevertheless I managed to build some display items, and take them to the shops. In no time orders started to come in from, actors, writers, TV presenters, drug dealers, pop-stars and porn-stars. Somehow I managed to produce, deliver and install them, but customer-satisfaction was at a low-level.

Sales were somewhat hindered by the general fear that a waterbed would burst. To try and overcome this Russell arranged for an interview with Radio Leicester at one of our stockists. He stood on a chair and jumped onto the bed, causing a tidal wave that split the mattress, flooded the floor and caused the ceiling to collapse. Waterbeds just didn't work well in Britain. There was a place for them in hot countries, for the avoidance of bed bugs and in hospitals to help with bed sores. Although they could be heated, it was hard to maintain the correct temperature in such a large volume of water..

We also started to sell sack chairs, also known as bean-bags; and huge cushions, like there was no tomorrow. I started to buy large quantities of second quality leatherette, and expanded-polystyrene beads. I bought some second hand industrial sewing-machines and set to work. The volume increased to the extent that I had to build a large hopper, with steps up the side, in order to fill the finished product. During one particularly windy night, several cubic yards escaped, causing blizzard conditions on the main A4 road outside, resulting in traffic restrictions.

There was a huge input of energy, activity, money, and creative thinking, but no forthcoming profits. The situation became considerably worse on the first of January 1974, when Prime Minister Edward Heath introduced emergency legislation, to conserve electricity during the miners strike. Shops, businesses, pubs and factories could only burn electricity for three days a week, on pain of a severe fine. If you couldn't do it by day-light or candle-light in the cold, then you couldn't do it at all.

One of the first things to happen was just about every candle in the country was bought by shops and pubs, as well as members of the general public. I saw an opportunity here and I started buying as much wax as I could, from various wholesalers. I employed several friends on a casual basis and, with some crude camping equipment, went into production. Selling candles at this time was easier than falling off a log, but sourcing enough wax was increasingly difficult. Eventually I decided to go to a direct source, and approached Shell in Liverpool. Shell would not negotiate on their minimum order, so I ordered a 20 ton load. The slightly-delayed delivery arrived on the second of March 1974, just five days before the lifting of the restrictions. Candles were unsaleable, and boxes of paraffin wax that had been left in the rain were also not desirable. Sometimes things just don't work out as you plan.

Meanwhile, the waterbed business is not going well. The returns are growing in line with the sales. Although we make everything clear to the customer at the outset, they often don't follow the instructions, resulting in more and more disputes. On one particular occasion, a woman tried to bring a bed back with a hole in it, caused by a cigarette. Russell refused to accept responsibility, so the woman sent her husband into the store, to buy a huge pile of cushions, paying by cheque, which he subsequently stopped.

The next day I received a phone call from a man, asking many complicated questions. Eventually, I asked him why he was asking all these questions, and he explained he was a reporter from the News Of The World, doing a story on the case of a leaking waterbed. When I found out he was writing everything down I hung up, too late though. The following Sunday, there was a picture of the woman on the front page of The News Of The World, naked, sprawled over the pile of cushions. I was quoted throughout the article. With 8.2 million copies sold that week, it really didn't help us at all. Shortly afterwards I reached a financial settlement with Russell, and left the business, and his boundless optimism, although we remained friends.

Unrecognised Genius.

I first met Kevin at a gathering at a friend's house. Apparently, he had been seeking me out, as he had some business he wanted to discuss with me. He said, "I have invented some brilliant things, and have some good ideas, but I seem unable to make any business sense out of them." I said, "What type of things?" He said, "Well I have already started producing one of the first *answerphones* that is available to the public. It uses a *compact cassette* to record the incoming messages, which is a new idea. It is very easy to use, and could become quite normal to have one sitting by your phone." I said, "It sounds exciting." He said, "Yes, and that is just the start. I have also invented what may be the first digital thermometer."

I said, "How does that work, roughly." He said, "Some eight years ago, the electronic thermometer, which relied on electronic sensors, instead of mercury or alcohol, was invented. I have just integrated this technology with the new digital technology, using simple LEDs." I said, "Sounds like a product with great potential."

He continued, "The very latest thing I am working on is a sensor system for cars, that will give an audible sound, if the driver gets too close to another car in front. Four sensors are fitted to the front bumper of a car. They emit a high-frequency sound wave which is reflected off a vehicle in front. The closer the car; the quicker the sound will bounce back; the closer together the beeps sound." I said, "That sounds great too."

He said, "My problem is that I can't get enough people to work on my *answerphone* production line; I can't find anyone interested in my *digital thermometer*; I can't find the money to finance it all. This is why I want you to get involved. What do you think?" I said, "I think I have something to offer. Yes, I'm in."

At the first opportunity I went to see him at his house in Caversham, from where he ran his business. There were a couple of *heads* in the dining room, fiddling around with some wires on a board. They both looked bored and depressed. Looking around the room, I could see various boxes of resistors and transistors; rolls of different coloured wire; plastic and metal boxes for the individual finished product; a few electrical, soldering, and carpentry tools. Apparently there was an endless demand for these, from a large electronic public company. They just could not keep up with the demand, so we were challenged with increasing production.

Firstly I asked Kevin to design a simple-to-use template, using a square of plywood, nails and different coloured marker pens. I then employed Ken, to make up 40 templates for each of the different types of *wire harness*. I made contact with all my friends and acquaintances, whom I thought might be interested in some cash-work that could be done in the daytime, evenings or nights. To my amazement about fifty reported for work, within the first couple of days. Some needed the money while others just wanted to be in on the scene.

We took over the sitting room and two of the bedrooms for different parts of the production. In no time, there was something that looked like a production line. While I stoked up the production, Kevin continued with his new developments, as well as performing the role of quality-control, which was really testing and fault finding. I would make regular bi-weekly trips to the customer in London, to deliver the finished items, receive payment and restock on the branded elements, like the boxes. With this healthy cash-flow under my belt, I applied and received a sufficient over-drought from my Bank, Barclays International.

I performed a time and motion study, and worked out a labour price for each component part of the device, and put it into practice. The staff were really happy, being able to choose when and for how long they worked. They liked the conditions: being able to work with their friends, play loud music, smoke dope, and get a free takeaway after they had worked more than 12 hours. One guy in particular, was able to work at such a high speed he was making a fortune. It was going really well and I had success in my sights.

The more production increased, the more staff I took on, and the more the curtains in this middle-class street of semi-detached houses twitched. As James arrived back with the take-away, about ten on a Friday evening, there was banging and shouting at the front door. When I answered it, in burst three police officers and about 20 uniforms, announcing they were from Reading Drugs Squad.

They were completely flabbergasted. Thinking they had smashed some kind of a drugs ring, and expecting to find buying and selling of drugs; wholesale quantities of drugs, cash, scales, the odd writhing, naked, under-age, drug-crazed girl, or, worst still, two homosexuals. What did they find? They found 37 young, dope-smoking, long-haired men and women, focused and dedicated to building a complicated piece of electronic apparatus. We turned off the music as requested. To break the stunned silence, I asked the officer in charge, "Do you mind if we eat our takeaway before it gets too cold?" He said, "Yes, but no one is to move from their seat."

This gave him a bit of a break, to communicate with his Superior on his radio. There was an amount of *Charlie, Foxtrot, Tango;* followed by a *10.99* (Send urgent back-up); *belay that*, I'll call you back; *10:4* (Message received). Then they systematically searched everyone and, almost without exception, everyone was either smoking a joint, had dope in their pockets or a bag under the work table. They then started taking down names, which resulted in a list sounding like the *1960s Rock Hall of Fame.* Addresses weren't much better with some claiming to live in an area of Reading called *Zinzania* and others on a working holiday from their home in Turkmenistan. The police collected all the dope they could find, placed it in a bag and left. That was the last we ever heard of the incident. Someone must have decided prosecution would not be in the public interest.

Clearly it was not possible to carry on production from Kevin's home. Fortunately, I still had the property that I had used for the manufacturing of the waterbeds, so we moved straight in there. The company we were supplying these answerphones to, were getting increasingly agitated, saying they needed to have a blueprint of the product, and understand how it works. They said they needed this information for various patent issues, guarantees and repairs. It seemed reasonable so I managed to convince Kevin to spend over a week working with their chief engineer, transferring the design from Kevin's head to paper.

On the day that they achieved their aim, the Managing Director turned to me and said, "Okay Paul, we now have what we need, so we will be bringing all the production in-house, and reducing the unit cost by 70%." I said, "But we had an agreement that you would not do that." He said, "Well you have just learnt a valuable lesson." I said, "What is that then? Not to trust the word of someone that is employed by a large corporation?" They were foolish really, because Kevin could have further developed it, so that the user could obtain messages remotely. I admit, not as foolish as me though.

Although kind in nature, Kevin was a very difficult character to deal with, like most geniuses. I was not up to the job of managing him in the way he needed to be managed. He would spend most of his time joking around, then, in a burst of brilliance, design something truly groundbreaking. Out of acute frustration, I resorted to verbal bullying, to try and get the best results for both of us, something I am ashamed of now I reflect upon it. A true genius, I wish him success and happiness in the future, but I have to move on.

The Road to Goulimine.

I had some British Overseas Airline vouchers that Russell had given me, so I suggested to Sonia that we take a holiday, and look for the source of the Goulimine beads. She agreed, always happy to go back to Morocco, and flying would be a real luxury. We flew to Casablanca and transferred to the Marrakesh Express train. After a pleasant break in Marrakech we commenced our odyssey by taking the bus going south. Soon after leaving Marrakech we started climbing the High Atlas Mountains.

The bus was old and rickety with no glass in the windows. It was mostly filled with women and the occasional ancient man and goat. Most of the women had orange peel covering their noses, like a mask, presumably to deal with the unwanted smells. This is the first time I had seen a herd of goats up a tree. This is actually quite a common practice in this area, and works well for the goats, who seem to enjoy eating the leaves; and for the shepherd, who can just doze in the shade of the tree, knowing his flock is safe. Looks odd though.

The bus heaved its way up the mountain, sometimes with only inches between the bald tyres, the edge of the broken up road surface and a sheer drop. We had been travelling for about four hours and were already tired from the noise, vibration and dirty from the black exhaust fumes coming back into the bus through the unglazed windows. Suddenly all the women on the bus broke out into ululation. This is the first time I had heard this strange, high pitched, long wavering trilling sound and it gave me goose pimples. Apparently ululation happens to release happy or sad emotions when the right words are not available. In this case it was because we had reached the highest point on this mountain road as indicated by the sign saying *Tizi n Test 2100m*. Sonia said, "I recognize that name. Haven't we been here before?" I replied, "Wow! Look at those snow capped mountains."

We arrived in Taroudant, early evening, and checked into one of the few hotels we could find. Liking the look of the place, we decided to stay for two nights, to give us a chance to explore the city. Oddly, as we were mooching around the town, the locals would call out: "Welcome to Marrakech Grandma." When we asked the hotel owner, he said Taroudant was called the *Grandmother of Marrakesh,* because it looks quite similar, being totally encased in a huge protective wall.

The next day we explored this market town, by tracing the six kilometre wall and its nine gates. It is unusual to find a town completely contained within the wall. The only activity outside the wall is a small tannery, only selling stuff for camels, like saddle bags, spider harness parts, and other equipment for desert work. Taroudant is a market town on the road to the desert, so camels are an important form of transport here, and much prized. Hardly surprising for a beast that can cover 50 miles a day, and do that every day for a month, without water. A Dromedary can stand up to eleven feet to the shoulders, and a female, at peak lactation, can yield up to 20 pounds of milk a day. They are wonderful to ride, with their slow side to side movement, but you must lean back when you mount up, or you'll be thrown off.

Since it was only a couple of hours to Agadir, we decided to go with a shared taxi, and enjoy a bit of comfort. We arrived in Agadir mid-morning. I was immediately surprised to find nothing but new buildings. I was further surprised to hear them talk in a strange tongue, which I later found out was called Tamazigh. Tamazigh is the language of the Amazigh people, who make up more than half of the 60,000 population of Agadir. The language belongs to the Afro-Asiatic family, and is related to Ancient Egyptian. This explains why their calendar starts at 943 BC, which is when Shoshenq ascended the throne of Egypt. Agadir is regarded as the capital for the Amazigh people. During their New Years Celebration, known as the Yennayer, on 13th January (1st January in the Julian calendar), the town is kicking with their dance, traditional clothes, cultural food and music.

I have come across the Amazigh people before, in Algeria, and my intrigue only deepens. They are believed to have started moving west from the Nile Valley, around 2000 BC, towards the Maghrib, which is the Atlas Mountains and coastal plain of Morocco. The women pose a timeless beauty, with their golden coloured skin, that seems to shimmer as they walk. Every element of their clothing contains a woven story of their ancient past, and their jewellery of silver and enamel are symbols of their wealth and status. I could go on, but I will just say that it is their captivating, ethereal eyes that I found so mysterious.

The city has a rich past, including Portuguese occupation from 1504 to 1541. Unfortunately, in 1960, there were two earthquakes, a tidal wave, and a fire, that completely destroyed the city, its Roman and Portuguese buildings, and wiped out a fifth of the population. This explained all the new buildings. We made our way to the beach looking for a hotel. This was not difficult since the beach was lined with brand new, modern hotels. We checked into what looked like the most luxurious one, and paid something under two pounds for a suite. I loved it. The level of service, the food, coffee, and the location being right on a wonderful sandy Atlantic beach. We were having a few days of something like a normal holiday, although it was strange to rub shoulders with people from England that had just got off a plane to start their package holiday.

After a few wonderfully relaxing days, we headed off by bus. The plan was to go to Goulimine, locate the source of the fabled *Goulimine* beads, buy as many as possible, import into England, sell them and become minted. What could go wrong? Since it was less than two hours to get to Tiznit, we again chose a shared taxi. Tiznit is a pretty little walled town, surrounded by irrigated fields of dates and vegetables, but we decided to pass through it and go directly to our next destination, Goulimine, since it was not much further.

Goulmine was a pleasant surprise. It is a pretty little oasis town at the foot of the Atlas Mountains. The population of less than 15,000, mostly Amazigh speaking people, make their living from agriculture. The first thing I noticed was miles of lush evergreen date palms following the river. I found out the river is called Ghris, it is seasonal and probably accounts for why Goulimine is so verdant. With the clean desert air, green environment and the wonderful clear starry night sky, it really is a pleasant place to spend some time.

We checked into a fairly clean and friendly hotel, and almost immediately, left the room to explore the town. We found Inourir Square, which seemed to be the focal point of the town, and settled down for a mint tea. There was a lot of energetic activity in and around the square. We sat and watched business being transacted, farmers thrashing their cereal and street performers in the form of jugglers and acrobats. Mixed in with the general mass of souls was a large contingent of white people dressed in amazing colourful clothes. I later found out they were the *Ait Marghad* people, famed for their poetry and performances at the summer festival of mysticism and spirituality. They share this festival with the Jews of *Ighrem,* and a Sufi group of dark skinned Berbers, called *Ismkhan-Gnawa.*

As people came up to us and engaged in conversation, I started to make enquiries about the Goulimine beads. No one seemed to know anything about them. I tried asking the traders, still nothing. Eventually I found an educated man with a good command of English, and asked him, "Where can I buy *Goulimine* beads?" He said, "What are they?" I showed him a postcard depicting the product. He said, "This is spelt *Goulmine* whereas my town is spelt Goulmima, or sometimes even Guelmim but never *Goulimine*." When Sonia came back from her wander around a jewellery shop, she said, "Any luck?" I replied, "I am afraid we have come to this pretty jewel of a place because of a spelling mistake." We stayed for two nights and really enjoyed it.

I was relating this story to a Frenchman, staying in the same hotel as us. He said, "While I was staying in Venice, I saw a shop with a large selection of Goulmima beads. The shop was not busy, so I asked the owner where they came from. He said, 'They were made, mostly in Venice, using a process called millefiori. Sticks of different coloured glass are melted together to give this particular design. They were manufactured in huge quantities around the 15th century, for traders to take to Africa. They were used mostly to trade for slaves or precious metals. Often they were taken out in empty slave ships as ballast. I have always known them as Salve Beads or Trade Beads, but you are telling me Goulmima is on a caravan crossroads, so I can see your logic in calling them Goulmima Beads."

We had one final stop on our odyssey, the last town in Morocco, Tan-Tan. Again we took a shared taxi as there seemed to be no other way of getting there. It is not very far but it took most of the day. Arriving at Tan-Tan was a bit of a shock, as we passed many failed attempts to try to keep the desert out, by planting row after row of trees, all of which had died. The first thing I noticed was goats, with their udders completely covered in cloth, and secured with a padlock. The population of 10,000 was much smaller than I had anticipated, and many people seemed to be begging or just standing around doing nothing. I saw a dried up river bed housing hundreds of tents, with many attempts to dig wells in the desperate hope of finding water, for themselves, and their emaciated looking livestock. There was clearly a water crisis in this place.

On top of this water crisis, Tan-Tan is also in disputed territory. Morocco has long claimed The Spanish Sahara as its own, and a bitter dispute has erupted, though thankfully Spain and Morocco have not come to blows over it. Why anyone would want it is a mystery to me. What would they do with it anyway? It's just sand, unless there is something under the ground that they haven't told me about.

There were not many hotels to choose from, and they all looked grim. The first one we tried had a grubby looking room, available at a cost of less than ten bob. We were informed there was no running water, and that we would have to buy that separately. We tried what looked like the best of a bad bunch, and the owner informed me, his inn was the only one in town that had running water, but the cost was over £5. More that ten times the price of the one without water, and well over our budget. We opted for the first one, on the basis that we would not be staying long.

We immediately left our dirty and depressing room, and headed for the town square. We found one of the very few cafes, and ordered a Coca-Cola, since it looked like the only safe thing to drink. We sat outside and watched the activity in the square. There were a lot of emaciated sheep and goats, wandering about; some market stalls selling poor looking vegetables, attempts at street entertainment, that would be funny, if they weren't so tragic. Begging seemed to be something that anyone would turn their hand to, if they saw a European, which was probably not often.

One rather odd thing we spotted was the occasional man in western attire, wandering around holding a transistor radio, tape recorder, toaster, or other electrical equipment. I asked one of the locals what this was about. He said, "My town is on the edge of the Sachel region of the Sahara Desert. It has not rained there for more than twelve years so people are coming into towns like mine looking for work and food. To try and save my town, and allow some commerce, our Gracious King Hassan made my town a duty free port. This means lorries come from the north, with these modern electrical items, and people travel down, also from the north, to buy these same things."

We couldn't find any reason to stay for long. This was the last town on our tour, the last town in Morocco, the last town before the desert, and maybe, the last place on earth. Apart from anything else, we had to get back to Tangiers, in time for our plane. We travelled pretty much non-stop. Sonia said, "Please no, not Tizi n' Test again." I said, "No lets' not. We can go to Agadir, and see if we can pick up our flight from there." That is one thing that did work out, and we arrived safely home on May Day 1973, sadly without *Goulimine Beads*. I would have to try something else to get *minted*.

Reverse Property Development.

I had a strange idea about house ownership. I believed that all houses needed to be improved, in order to increase their value. Improvements could be made by ripping out the old stuff, and replacing it with new, more modern stuff. It didn't matter how much money you spent on it, because you would always get that back in the long run. Using a credit card to pay for it was also fine, since any money spent on a house was a good investment. Credit cards were beginning to become available, so I applied for, and received one. I was ready to go.

My first project was to rip out all the Edwardian skirting board and architrave, and replace it with a modern profile one. My next project was to rip up all the carpets and underlay. They were not worn, or dirty, but they were definitely of an old fashioned design. I would replace them with, well actually, by now I was up to the limit on my credit card, so replace it with some Moroccan blankets for now. Moroccan blankets made passable curtains as well. Next came a complete redecoration, so I bought a gas flame-thrower, to burn off the old lead-based paint. Sadly, as I proceeded to burn off the paint on the windows, most of the panes cracked. I could deal with that later.

I now took a moment to stand back, and survey my work. The new skirting and architrave was in place, but unpainted. Sonia seemed to think they were not in keeping with the character of the property, but I still had an open mind. The doors, windows, and bannisters had a rather unpleasant looking charred-effect, but I could deal with that later as well. The floors were mostly bare wood, but they could clearly be improved by painting them, until funds permitted the purchase of new carpets and underlay. Well at least I had made a start.

One wet Wednesday evening, over dinner, I suggested the living room and dining room could be improved by knocking down the dividing, supporting, wall, thus creating one large open-plan space. I felt the need to crack on with the house-improvements, since we had already owned it for more than three weeks. While Sonia cleared away the dishes, I set to, with a large sledgehammer. By bedtime I had most of the wall down, as Sonia looked on aghast. I was on a roll, so the next evening after work, I thought, "Why not have a hatch to the kitchen?"

Again I took some moments to stand back and admire my handiwork, and consider my next move. In a blinding flash it came to me. I needed to remove the fireplace in the old dining room; rip out the stove with the back-boiler that provided all the hot water, from the sitting room. Never mind that we had no hot water, and no means of heating any rooms in the house. I could deal with that later, in order of priority. While drinking a cup of tea, and looking at the ragged, blackened holes, where the fires used to be earlier in the evening, I had another creative flash of inspiration. The holes were ideally suited to contain two large sound speakers. We would have a truly modernised house then.

On Friday evening Sonia said, "Let us go out for a drink tonight, rather than continue with the house attack? Perhaps tomorrow I could get my Dad around to look at the ceiling. It is beginning to sag from where the structural wall has been removed. It would be interesting to hear his opinion." We did go down the pub and had a few pints. When we returned, again we could not find the house. I planted a huge sunflower in the front garden, to make sure we were never confronted by this embarrassing situation again.

On Saturday Stanislav visited us on his bike. He was horrified I had taken down the wall, and not put any supports in place.

We rushed over to his house, and picked up some acrow-props that would support the ceiling, upstairs-floors, and upstairs-walls, and possibly the roof, until a steel joist could be purchased and put in place. He did ask why I had destroyed the walls, ripped out the heating and hot water system, changed the lovely joinery and torn up the carpets. I tried to explain it to him but clearly he was too old to understand the benefits of property development.

The pace of my development project became somewhat slower, as I got deeper and deeper in debt. My spirits sank, I caught body lice. and for the first time in my life, I fell into a depression. To try to shake it off, I threw myself on a train and travelled to the Isle of Skye. Sadly distance would not kill the *black dog,* so I returned a week later and took to my bed, which incidentally was a rather grubby mattress on the floor.

After a visit to my doctor, and a prescription for some heavy duty insecticide, I managed to kill the lice, but not the *black dog*. In another attempt to get my head together, I thought I would walk from Reading to Henley-on-Thames, along the riverbank. I set off quite late in the day, and consequently only got a short way before dusk. This turned into a bit of a nightmare. Most of the way, there was no footpath. I was trudging through boggy fields, climbing through thorny hedgerows, jumping over barbed wire, and trying to avoid fields of frisky bullocks and a bull.

By the time I reached Henley it was nearly midnight. I called on friends, to see if I could get a bed for the night, but they were either away or fast asleep. I saw a light in the window of the ground floor flat, and since I had been there before, and knew the girl that lived there a little, I knocked on the door. She answered the door and invited me in. She fed me, we smoked some dope, listened to music, shared a bottle of wine, then we shared a bed for the night. In the morning I left.

What had I done? My attempt to lift my depression by going for a long walk had gone horribly wrong. I had betrayed my wife. I could have kept it a secret; she would never have found out; but that would have been a double-betrayal. I told her, and she disappeared. I was distraught. I went mad looking for her, trying every place I thought she might be. I even drove as far as Wales to find her. I was standing on a beach, watching a tsunami hurtling towards me.

After a week she returned home, bearing a gift of a money box with, *For That Rainy Day,* inscribed on the side. She had accompanied John on his sales trip to Cornwall. I made a deep, heartfelt vow to myself ,and to her, that I would never betray her again. I knew that wasn't enough, I knew that it would take time to rebuild the trust, but we both knew that there was enough love there for us to do it. Still I was depressed.

Russell kindly let us use his house in Wales, and we stayed there for a long-weekend. We talked quite a bit, but mostly we sat in silence, on the covered porch, watching the farm cat go about his business, listening to the rain falling on the corrugated iron barn roof, and the barn door banging in the wind. We drove home, feeling we would get over it, but with me still feeling depressed.

The following Monday morning Sonia went off to work as I lay in bed. She had left the radio on, oddly tuned to Radio Three, at high volume. I started listening. I didn't know at the time that I was listening to Beethoven's Symphony No. 6 Pastoral. It lifted my spirits, and within hours I was on my feet and ready to face the world again. After a month, I had won the battle and slain the *black dog*. It was dead, gone, finished, over.

I took stock of the situation. In spite of a rising property market, I had actually managed to reduce the value of our house; I was hopelessly in debt; business was not going very well at all; our home was cold and uncomfortable to live in and I had more work to do on the house than I could possibly comprehend. There were two of us in this and I knew, deep down, we would get through it. Stanislav came to the rescue, with his knowledge, tools and positive attitude.

Over the next few months, with Stanislav's help and guidance, I managed to install central heating and a hot water system, replace broken and cracked window glass, redecorate the house, and generally transform it into a habitable home. The house was respectable enough to have some friends living with us as lodgers, which helped with the raging 24% inflation, and enormous 8% mortgage costs. I still had a pile of debts, but I felt sure something would come along to help with this. Meanwhile I needed to get on the road and start selling again, when I was back from my holiday.

A Diplomatic Incident.

I hadn't heard from Russell for some time, when he telephoned me out of the blue. He said, "I bumped into my old friend Billy. You may know him, he has a boot shop in Kings Road. Anyway, a Lebanese diplomat wandered into his shop and asked if he could sell some dope from the shop. Billy wasn't interested, so he thought of me, and I thought of you." I said, "Thank you for thinking of me. Yes, I will certainly give it a go." He said, "Okay, I'll pass on your number to Billy."

We usually buy cannabis from friends or friends of friends who have recently travelled to countries like Thailand, Turkey, Morocco, Nepal, or India. They will have brought it back concealed within their personal belongings, or opt to ship it home using clever disguises, like wooden carved ornaments, hollowed-out books, musical boxes, or rolled-up rugs. I had often wondered why there was always Lebanese blond available, yet I had never met anyone who had been to Lebanon.

A couple of days later, Billy did phone me. He said, "I don't think we have met ,but Russell says I can trust you, and that is good enough for me." I said, "Thank you for the compliment. Yes, you can trust me." He said, "I met this really nice young guy at a party, and I said I would help him find someone to sell his dope. Russell says you are interested." I said, "Yes, I would be happy to meet him." He said, "Can you meet him on Thursday evening?" I said, "That sounds fine." He said, "Okay I'll call you back."

Billy called me back shortly after our first phone call, and said, "Okay, I've arranged for you to meet him at 7:30 tomorrow evening, outside the Brigham Young University, in Palace Court. You will be able to recognize him by the brown leather suitcase he will be carrying. You won't let me down Paul, will you?" I said, "Of course I will not Billy. Speak soon."

I arrived at the appointed time and met the man, he never said his name. He was small, smartly dressed, of Middle-Eastern appearance, and extremely affable. He said, "I work at the Lebanese Embassy, just around the corner. I have been obliged to do this because my Mother needs a life-saving kidney operation. I have never used my *diplomatic bag* in such a way before." I said, " I am sorry to hear about your Mother. I hope I can help." He said, "I know I can trust you, so here you are." Then he handed me the suitcase. I said, "I will send a message through Billy, when I have sold it, but it may take some weeks." He said, "No problem, I will not worry."

With that I took the case, walked back to my car and drove home. When I got home I opened the case for the first time. It was full of 50, one pound, blocks, of finest Blonde Lebanese Hash, individually wrapped in muslin cloth. Blonde Lebanese Hash is one of the best products on the market. The cannabis plants are grown organically over two seasons, about an eight month cycle. Once the plants have flowered they are carefully harvested by hand. The process involves removing and processing the trichomes, or resinous glands into a concentrated form. This is done by sifting the mature flowers through a series of sieves until it ends up as a heap of resinous-powder. This powder is then compressed and heated to form flat blocks. All done without using any chemicals or additives.

Blonde Lebanese Hash has many medicinal properties and health benefits. Its higher concentration of THC, acts as an antioxidant and anti-inflammatory agent, providing strong psychoactive effects, and helping manage anxiety, stress, and skin diseases. It also acts as a neuroprotectant, protecting and multiplying brain cells, improving memory, and maintaining cognitive health. With its higher THC content, it can effectively reduce pain, inflammation, and nausea, making it a practical treatment option, particularly for cancer patients experiencing chemotherapy side-effects.

It's also fun to use with no known side effects or negative connotations. We know regular use of alcohol, even in modest amounts, kills thousands every year. It can also promote street and domestic violence and is responsible for many, often fatal, car accidents. No question, millions die worldwide, through the use of tobacco. There is a growing body of evidence that ultra-processed foods can develop obesity, sometimes also resulting in death. Yet no one in a recorded history of millennia has ever died from the use of cannabis. Anyone that has ever been stoned will know that the last thing they will do is jump into a car and drive through town at 70 mph; 15 mph is about the limit when you are stoned. Nor will a stoned person pick a fight with anything more substantial than an electric toaster.

Still we continue to treat cannabis like a dangerous drug, and continue this war on a vegetable. I expect it will soon become legal, or at least decriminalised, possibly starting in countries with a more liberal outlook like Holland, Canada and Scandinavia. I will predict that by the end of the 1970s it will be widely used, and legal throughout most of the Western World.

I unpack the suitcase and place the contents in an empty typewriter case, and put it in the loft. I then phone a friend in Norfolk, one in Henley and a couple in Reading. Each buys a one pound block, known as a *weight,* to try. The price is reasonable and the quality is so superior that they all return the next day for more. Within less than a week I have sold it all. I count the money into blocks of £1000 and place the agreed sum of £130 per weight into the brown leather suitcase. I phoned Billy and asked him to arrange another meeting; same place; same time; same day of the week.

When I attended the meeting, this pleasant man shook my hand, and I gave him the suitcase. He took it and thanked me warmly. There was no question of him checking it; I never knew his name; he never knew mine. This was a business transaction between two gentlemen, and that is how good business is always done. I later found out from Billy, his title was First Secretary of the Lebanese Embassy, responsible for economic affairs. As such he had a compartment in the diplomatic bag for business related items. In the case of the Lebanese Embassy, they apparently often sent over diplomatic bags that were in fact containers.

A Strange Incident In Gretna Green.

To complete the business model we bought two transit vans. John and I would drive to London on Saturday, and spend the day visiting our growing network of wholesalers, most of whom were Kenyan-Asian, Indian or Jewish. On Sundays we would sort all the stock and divide it in two, before carefully reloading our vans. We would then work out a price list and Sonia would type it out. Monday morning we would set off on our week-long sales trip, with the aim of selling everything. We had divided the country into six areas which we would each visit in turn, meaning every customer would be seen every three weeks.

It was a really good formula that appeared to have found a gap in the market. Retailers loved the idea of being able to buy the right, up-to-date product, at a reasonable price, without having to leave their shops. It was also a wonderful opportunity for me to visit just about every corner of the United Kingdom. I would always try to make a point of using the evenings to explore. I would try not to pass interesting places without at least a cursory look around. Of course there would be surprise events and chance meetings as one would expect, driving so many miles, but I could never wait to get back home again on a Friday evening.

After one particularly successful trip to Scotland, when I had been able to sell almost everything, I did have a little adventure. I was driving south on Friday evening, when I pulled over to reorganise the back of my van. I tightly wedged the jeans I had been unable to sell, into one column, behind the driver's seat, to stop them floating around in the back. I drove across the border into England and stopped at a service station, not far from Gretna Green. After eating, I set off again to rejoin the road heading South. The road was dug up with many diversion signs, as they were laying new curbs. Unfortunately

I had rejoined the correct road but was now heading north again.

Shortly afterwards, I saw a curb stone spanning the road. I did not have the time to stop, so I hit it, causing all four tyres to deflate, and the van to roll over, end to end. As I was rolling, I saw my life in front of me, and everything was in slow motion, just as I had heard happens. As I looked around me, I could see all the glass shattering, and the metal of the van gently folding in on me. I could see the roof was touching the passenger seat, and the windscreen had gone. I was hanging upside down in complete silence.

I undid my seat belt, and landed on my head, on the inside of the roof, before escaping the vehicle completely, standing back in case the fuel tank exploded. I could now see that the jeans I had hated because I could not sell them, had saved my life. Because I had packed them in so tightly, they had protected the area around the driver's seat. Within minutes a police car arrived with a junior officer and the Station Sergeant. They checked I was okay and radioed for a recovery vehicle to quickly clear this major road.

A recovery crane arrived and set about righting the vehicle. As the crane lifted my van up, all the stuff in the driving compartment fell out. There was all my picnic gear, vegetarian necessities, sponge bag, bread knife, box of liquorice assortments etc. all tumbling out and falling in a heap. When it seemed like it had finished falling out, the sergeant looked up into the cab, and my little dope pipe fell out, hitting him on the head.

The Station Sergeant said, "What is this?" I said, "I don't think we need to worry about this, officer." He didn't agree, and decided to take me to the police station, to give me a strip search. It didn't take long for them to find my small lump of dope. His next step was to call for a police car, to transport me to Dumfries Police Station, where they were able to accommodate me for the night.

It all became rather bizarre. The two police that came to collect me were very amiable and friendly. Surprisingly, they were very pro-cannabis smoking. The driver said, "We work in some pretty rough areas. We always find a big improvement in behaviour, if young people turn from drink to cannabis. All the aggression seems to evaporate, and they stop fighting. It's a bonus that no one ever died from taking cannabis." Just as we were driving through the centre of Dumfries, he pulled over, wound down the window, and called out, "Over here Jimmy." This rather rough looking guy walked over, and the policeman said, "Are you keeping your nose clean tonight?" Jimmy replied, "You know me. It's peace and love now."

When I got to the station, I traipsed in carrying my possessions, which I had been holding on my lap, in the back of the police car. Unbelievably, they had not even thought to take away my ten inch bread knife. The Custody Sergeant took my fingerprints. He said, "Why are your fingers so rough?" I said, "I have been doing a lot of decorating at home." He said, "Me too." There followed quite a long conversation on decorating and general DIY, before I was put in a cell, pending an appearance in front of the Procurator Fiscal, in the morning.

When I arrived at the courthouse, I was appointed a defence lawyer. We sat down to discuss the case. He had never taken on a drug case before, so was looking to me for guidance. We walked into the courtroom, and the prosecution read out the case against me. "You are charged with being in possession of a dangerous drug." My defence lawyer turned to me and asked, "It's not dangerous, is it?" I said, "No." He said, "My client pleads guilty, but I must stress that there is no evidence that cannabis is dangerous."

Prosecution: "Exhibit A, Is this cannabis?" Actually, it was of such poor quality, it may not have been cannabis at all. I was not prepared to wait in a cell for a laboratory result, so I said, "Yes." He said, "Where did you buy it?" I said, "Piccadilly Circus." He said, "I thought so, there are a lot of drugs sold there. Exhibit B, what is this?" I said, "A *Liquorice Allsort* Your Honour." He said, "Is there anything you would like to tell this court?" I said, "I had been working in Scotland, selling jeans, and I was travelling back to my home and Wife, when I had this accident. It can be a very lonely life, staying in hotels every night. I sometimes smoke cannabis, which helps." Then came a really awkward moment when he said, "If you were on your way home, why were you travelling north?" I could not answer that. The Procurator Fiscal said, "Fifty pound fine, to be paid before the end of the month. Case closed."

I had used up my *Get Out Of Jail Free* card, and come close to death. Perhaps it was time for me to grow up a little. I had a good home, and I was in a loving marriage. It is true, I had an almost insurmountable pile of debts, but I felt sure something would turn up, perhaps in the next book. Still I felt something was missing. I made a cup of tea, turned on the central heating, yes, *central heating,* and said to Sonia, "Do you want to have a baby?" She said, "Yes okay."

A Study On Where Time Goes.

It is August 2023. The United Kingdom is in the middle of one of the most miserable summers for years while the rest of the planet experiences the serious effects of climate change. Southern Europe and North America is in its third heat wave with temperatures regularly exceeding 44c; a portion of

Canada, Portugal, spain, Croatia, Italy and Greece is on fire last night Palm Springs in California was inundated with more rain in one hour than the total of all the rain that has ever fallen on the city since Jack Summers first set up his stagecoach station on the Bradshaw Trail in 1862. That is just a glimpse of what we are doing to our planet. My early travels cost the planet almost nothing. More often than not I was taking a spare seat in a vehicle that was going my way. At worst I would be taking up a seat on a train or a bus.

In the intervening 50 years since my early travels many things have changed. More striking though are the things that have not changed. Morocco has experienced a boom in middle-class tourism with figures peaking at more than 10m. France provides the greatest numbers of European tourists by far, although they are sometimes resented. I well remember sitting in a cafe in Marrakech fairly recently and overhearing a French tourist suggest to the waiter that, without the years of French colonial rule Morocco would be an uncultured, uncivilised place. Unfortunately during the pandemic lockdowns the number of visiting tourists plummeted and have still not recovered.

Roads and railways have been much improved, the streets in the Royal Bazaar have been paved, small Chinese motorbikes are everywhere and almost everyone has a mobile phone. Jemaa el-Fnaa square is no longer a muddy *or dusty* patch of waste ground where buses stop and turn around while you grab a bite to eat from a stall. It is now a paved pedestrian area that comes alive at night to provide the tourist with places to eat and drink and buy their souvenirs. Still the acrobats, snake-charmers, Indian rope-trick con-merchants and henna tattooists ply their trade. The blind beggar's choir is still at the entrance to the kasbah and the hammans are doing good business.

Tan-Tan is no longer the last town in Morocco, or so their people say. Morocco long felt it had a claim over Spanish Sahara and in 1975 King Hassan ordered his so-called *Green March*. Typical of peace-loving Morocco 200,000 unarmed volunteers crossed the border to occupy Spain's territory. To avoid confrontation Spain relinquished its claim over the territory and it was renamed The Western Sahara. The locals wanted to be independent and not a part of Morocco so a guerilla war ensued. In 2020, as payback for formalising ties with Israel, the US recognised Morocco's sovereignty over

The Spanish Sahara, followed by Israel in 2023. Sadly the war continues.

Algeria did manage to break free of France thus avoiding the crushing poverty of central African states like Niger, Chad, Mauritania, Mali and Burkina Faso etc. that still suffer from French extraction. Now it is hydrocarbons, rare metals and uranium U-235 rather than slaves, ivory and gold. After abolition of the slave trade local slaves were recruited and their blood, sweat and tears was exported as food or minerals. Now the French Foreign Legion and other crack regiments patrol their realms, ostensibly for counterterrorism, stabilisation and peacekeeping, in reality protecting their interests and ensuring their debt interest is paid to date. Look at a map of Africa. To see the countries that are still being bled dry by France look for political instability, terrorism, illiteracy. These countries are French.

In Algeria oil and mining exports have dramatically improved the wealth and wellbeing of the population, increasing the average annual income from $250 when I first visited to $4275 now and life expectancy to 77 years. However with a population increase from 12m to 45m it suffers the enduring plague of Africa, almost one third of young people unemployed. Millions of young people, unable to follow their hopes and dreams hanging out with their mates with nothing positive to do. Somehow this beautiful, rich country never quite made it in the way I hoped and thought it would.

Twenty years after my last visit to Tunisia I found an opportunity to return with my young family. I found the country stable, prosperous, friendly and greener than I had remembered it. Although my children never knew it, I found myself standing with them outside the *Banque Al-Baraka* in Tabarka, the very same bank I had robbed. I thought "If I've got a list of twenty life changing moments that was one."

Sometime after my last visit to Libya Gaddafi came to power in a bloodless military coup in 1969 while King Idris1 was out of the country receiving medical treatment. I had felt the tension in Sirte at the time of my visit, which was his hometown. He was a popular leader with a stated aim of dealing with inequality, corruption and exploitation of natural resources by western powers. He sought to use Libya's oil resources for the benefit of his 6m people, something he largely achieved.

There is no doubt that he had a tight control over all aspects of life in Libya but he also founded the Basic People's Congress at a local level and the General People's Congress at a national level. He founded the Libyan Women's Union with the stated aim of improving women's rights. Legal reforms were introduced to raise the minimum age of marriage, grant women the right to initiate divorce and promote education and employment opportunities for women. There were also many infrastructure improvements with some huge civil engineering projects.

Of course we all know him as a monster. Interesting that it took his people 42 years to also conclude that he was a monster. In 2011 he was hunted down by his people in Sirte, where it all started. Found hiding in a sewer pipe he was shot in the head by a boy and his regime came to an end. Since that day there has been no coherent government, no peace, only chaos and confusion. But no monster.

When I first visited Egypt the population was 30m. I thought the country was full to capacity bearing in mind only some 10% of the land can support human life. Now the population is around 110m, all crammed into the same space. The eternal bountiful Nile helps with that. No surprise then that they would readily go to war to protect the upper reaches of the Blue Nile from any detrimental effects of the massive Grand Ethiopian Renaissance Dam.

I have returned to Egypt several times over the years as my interest in Ancient Egypt has grown. I can confirm first hand that the boys of Alexandria no longer wear striped pyjamas in the street. Strangely none of the locals have any knowledge of this ever being the case. This was not a figment of my imagination. I have discovered that President Gamal Abdel Nasser, implemented a system of socialist-style youth organisations. As part of this, boys were often required to wear uniforms that were reminiscent of the striped uniforms worn by prisoners in Nazi concentration camps during World War II.

A little over a century after it was first opened and 3 years after Katie and myself sat in the Royal Box, in the early morning of 28 October 1971 the great Khedivial Royal Opera House was completely destroyed by fire. Following a visit to Japan by President Hosni Mubarak, funds to build a new opera house were gifted by the nation of Japan. In October 1988 President Mubarak and Prince Tomohito of Mikasa, the younger brother of the Japanese Emperor, inaugurated the National Cultural Centre Cairo Opera House.

While I was in Greece in 1967 I experienced the tail-end of the coup that saw the military junta take power. There followed a horrible repressive period of authoritarian rule until a popular uprising in 1974 established the *Third Hellenic Republic* and democracy. In 1981 Greece joined the EU and in 2001 the Euro. What I find strange is that since joining, Greece has become hugely indebted to Germany. The debt is so great it has been necessary to instigate strict austerity cuts for years. I also find it strange that this debit has mainly been built up by buying tanks from Germany. Not just any tanks but the cutting edge Leopard 2A7V. They now have 1244 heavy battle tanks against 527 in France and 227 in the UK.

The Island of Hydra in the Aegean sea is a magical place. When I was first there in 1967 I had no idea who I was sharing this tiny island with. I had met Marrianne just before she left the island with her poet boyfriend Leonard. She had told me she was trying to convince him to sing his poetry but he was resisting as he didnt think he could sing. It was true Leonard Cohen could not sing but it did not matter, it was the poetry that did it.

I got to know the French artist Marceau a little. I had first met him when I was visiting the church of *Ai-Giannis the Fasting* on the Island. He invited us to his parties which were well known and famous throughout the artists community on Hydra. I may well have met Lawrence Durrell, Henry Miller, Norman Mailer or Le Corbusier but I would not recognise the names for a further twenty years. The Beatles spent time on Hydra a couple of months after we left and the Stones followed two years later. The Island was chosen by one of our travelling companions Manfred, because it is associated with the wonderful Austrian artist *Hundertwasser*. Hydra had a total population of about 2000 of which the artist's community made up ten percent. It was a privilege partying at Marceau's and getting to talk to so many interesting people yet have no idea who they are.

A chance meeting with Jean-Paul Sartre, the French existentialist philosopher in the lobby of the Cairo Hilton I do remember. I had no idea who he was at the time, I just remembered him because of his striking looks and huge presence. When he introduced himself I remember thinking how unfair it was that he should not only have my name, but my brother's as well.

The population of Istanbul has exploded from 1.5m which I first visited to 15.5m now. Although you will no longer see any flocks of goats being herded around the city centre some things have not changed. Hagia Sophia is still one of the most beautiful buildings I have ever laid eyes upon. Child labour seems to have disappeared from sight but I wonder if the old men hobbling around the Grand Bazaar with bowed legs were the rickets-inflicted child labourers of the past.

The last time I was in Istambule I spent some time asking around for the *Pudding Shop*. No one seemed to have heard of it until, finally, I asked an old man. He remembered it and directed me there. It is still owned by the same family and the one we used to call *laughing boy* still works there, although he is now in his late sixties. The notice board where we used to advertise "Munich £10" is still hanging in the same place. Now it is mostly covered in articles cut out of the Times Travel Supplement or The Guardian written by well known travel journalists. It morphed from a hippy-traveller meeting place to a tourist hot-spot after the 1978 book and film *Midnight Express*. Puddings are still great though.

Josip Broz Tito's health started declining in the 1970s by which time he had lost the ability to successfully govern Yugoslavia. Everyone was fearful about what would happen when their strong authoritarian leader died. So they kept him alive for as long as possible. They cut limbs off, operated on him and put him on life support and managed to keep him going until 1980. With no heir in such a diverse collection of countries Yugoslavia itself was put on life support. It finally died in the early 1990s along with an estimated 200,000 of its population. It made me think back to the disgusting way I saw besuited customers treating the small dark-skinned waiters. One of them didn't get the coffee he wanted so he actually slapped the waiter around the face. Looking back I can see what that was about now.

Freetown Christiania, the enclave inhabited and run by democratic anarchists, has now become the third most visited tourist attraction in Denmark. Although the residents have largely kept to their own rules - no private cars, weapons, hard drugs, fireworks, stolen goods, bulletproof clothing or bikers jackets - it has experienced its fair share of violence and even murder as various gangs of bikers attempt to gain control of the cannabis trade in Pusher Street. Recently the inhabitants have purchased the land and closed Pusher Street. All seems to be peaceful now. Which is more than can be said for Scandinavia as a whole. According to *Statista* Sweden has far more reported cases of sexual violence per capita than any other country in Europe, closely followed by Iceland, Norway and Denmark. Most happen in winter as the country and its people go into *The Tunnel*.

The war on drugs seems to be slowly grinding to a halt. It is no longer illegal to use cannabis in Canada, Uruguay, USA (some states), Mexico, Portugal, Netherlands, Germany, Austria, Israel, Jamaica, Colombia, South Africa, Malta, Thailand, Costa Rica, Belize, Luxembourg, Spain, Malta, Czech Republic, Argentina, Chile, Denmark, Croatia, Greece, Ireland, Macedonia, Philippines, Poland, India (some states), Puerto Rico, Ecuador, Italy, Turkey, Zimbabwe and more every week. For some strange reason the UK lags behind. The Government has repeatedly stated that they have no intention of legalising cannabis. The population of this country continues to shovel vast sums of money into the coffers of unpleasant and often violent gangs. Cannabis used to be imported into the United Kingdom in small quantities, often in travellers luggage. It was sold through a network of friends and acquaintances in a low key and harmless way. The money, resources and effort that has been put into this war on a harmless substance, over a period of half a century, is truly mind boggling. And it hasn't stopped yet!

The Family Dog shop was sold to the *Two Bills* who ran it as the *Plastic Passion* record shop. That is until they fell out and divided the already narrow shop into two record shops. *The Whole Earth Catalogue* was last published in 1971 having sold millions of copies. With its tips on spot welding, how to deal with a drug bust, install solar panels and get rid of body lice organically it is now widely accepted as a printed version of Google 35 years before Google was thought of.

Waterbeds never took off in this country and it is now near impossible to buy one, although ansaphones did have a good run for a few decades. I never did get to the bottom of the *Goulimine beads*.

Some words have gone out of fashion and more or less disappeared from common usage like: *freak* (cannabis user), *head* (cannabis user with long hair), *shit* (cannabis), *fuzz* (police), *far-out* (good), *spaced-out* (High on cannabis). Some have been adopted into common usage like: *cool, bread, groovy, pad, hassle.* While new words have been invented: *flipflop, backpack, hippy.*

At its zenith in the mid-19th century, the British East India Company possessed a formidable array of assets, including vast territorial holdings across the Indian subcontinent and Southeast Asia, immense wealth derived from trade monopolies and taxation, a well-equipped private army of over 250,000 personnel, an extensive network of trading infrastructure and ports, significant political influence through alliances with local rulers, monopolies on valuable commodities like opium, and legal rights and privileges granted by the British Crown.

After generations of growing greed and increasing extraction the Indian Mutiny happened at a cost of over 1m Indian lives. I mention this because, if the first responsibility of the British Government is to protect our land from hostile invaders across the Channel, they should extend the law to include hostile international corporations.

Enough said. It's been a gas.

Printed in Great Britain
by Amazon